Over the Next Horizon

Brian D. Ratty

Over the Next Horizon

In Retrospect

Brian D. Ratty

Sunset Lake Publishing
89637 Lakeside Ct.
Warrenton, OR 97146
503.717.1125
#93-1015196

First Edition published in May 2017
ISBN-13: 978-0692847459 (Sunset Lake Publishing)
ISBN-10: 0692847456
Create Space Title ID: 6551082
Printed in the USA

For my wife Tess and our three daughters; Shannon, Danean & Amy
Family is where life begins and love never ends

CONTENTS

My Books

The Early Years
The War Years
Tillamook Passage
Destination Astoria
Voyage of Atonement

Childhood Nickname: Tail Gunner

Brian and his sister Diane: 1949

Author's Note

One thing about time: it has been written about for centuries. We can't stop it, speed it up or slow it down. Some people have way too much of it, while others complain about its brevity when they look back upon their accomplishments. Time is just a commodity, like air and water and all we can do is watch it. Mother Teresa said it best: "Yesterday is gone. Tomorrow has not yet come. We have only today. So, let us begin."

Over the Next Horizon is all about time. It's a book of secrets told, new adventures, vivid characters, laughter, coming of age, and yes, failures: because failing is the key ingredient to success.

I was blessed to be born into a blue-collar family filled with love and understanding and fortunate enough, to ultimately marry into a second family with the same. Time can be stingy or generous, and I've always tried to use it looking forward, not back. The power of positive thinking is essential to good time management.

During my thirty five years in the media business, I received my share of accolades and awards. But never did I craft a Pulitzer Prize picture or film an Emmy winning commercial. It just didn't happen and it really didn't matter. Life was good and time bountiful.

With my love for history, I wrote my first book, *The Early Years*, almost twenty years ago. It was a rewarding half-a-decade process that led to four additional Historical Fiction novels. All of which proudly have won numerous literary awards. There is something about writing that is both fascinating and frightening. It is as if I've done this all before, in another life, and another time. I've sat in a Stockholm coffee house writing stories of the Vikings, or wandered the markets of Madrid telling tales of treasures found and conquering conquistadors. This feeling is as fleeting as time but as real as my words. This awareness reminds me that at my best, I am only a storyteller.

Now I find myself in a peculiar situation, I'm in the fourth act of my three act life. With any luck, when I grasp what's just over the next horizon, I'll have the commodity of time and the blessing of God to complete my journey through this wonderful life.

First Day At School

With writing tablet and pencil in hand, I went off to my first day at school in 1948. My first grade teacher, a family friend, was Mrs. Williams. She taught at the Multnomah Grade School (Multnomah, an Indian name, is a suburb of Portland, Oregon).

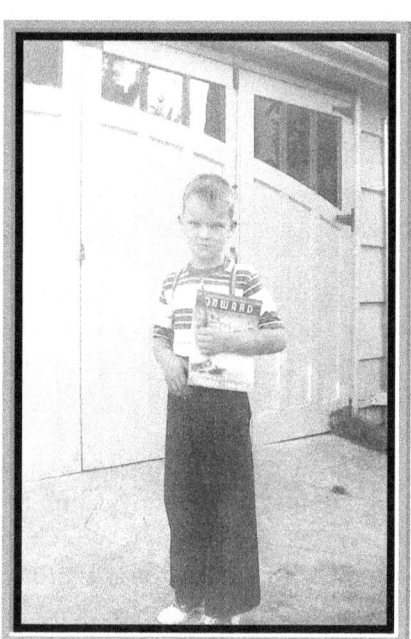

When I got to my classroom, she told us all to take a seat for roll call.

"As you hear your name, raise your hand and say 'here.' Johnny?"

A boy's arm went up. "Here."

"Mary?"

A girl's arm went up. "Here."

Finally she came to my name. "Brian?"

I did nothing.

Looking up from her roll book, she asked, "Brian, why didn't you raise your hand?"

"My name isn't Brian...it's O'Brian."

She rolled her eyes. "Who told you that?"

"Every time mommy calls me, she says, 'Oh, Brian, come here,' or 'Oh, Brian, don't do that!'"

Smiling, as she knew of my mischievous childhood, she answered, "No, here at school you're just Brian!"

And so it begins... †

Chapter 1
Tillamook People

Captain Robert Gray on Tillamook Bay 1788

The terrain of the Northwest Coastline is rugged and untamed, in many ways as forbidding as the natives that flourished on its shore. This narrow strip of land was home to dozens of different Indian nations. Just south of Tillamook Bay were many other nations, including the Siletz and the Siuslaw, while to the north were the Clatsop and Chinook tribes. Unlike most inland Indians, these nations didn't nomadically follow game or move with the seasons. Instead, they stayed close to the bays and the sea, establishing permanent homes and villages.

Within each Indian nation there were tribes, and within these tribes there were bands, and within these bands there were different clans. Each nation lived to the dictates of the resources Mother Nature provided, and their ability to hunt and gather food.

When Captain Robert Gray discovered Tillamook Bay in 1788, the Tillamook nation numbered roughly 2,200 natives. These people lived in nine different villages, from the Nestucca River in the south to the Nehalem Bay in the north. The largest Tillamook village was Kilharhurst, which occupied the land that is the present-day site of Garibaldi, Oregon. The river next to this village was called Kilharnar, known today as the Miami River. This village had about fifty lodges and five hundred inhabitants.

Over time, the Tillamooks assumed most of the customs, habits and dress of their powerful neighbors to the north, the Chinooks. Although both nations spoke the Salish language, their dialects were so different that, when they talked, they had to sign, as well. This was not unusual for coastal Indians, as each nation might speak a different tongue derived from the same general language.

The Killamucks, as some people called the Tillamooks, bore a likeness, in looks and dress, to other coastal nations. They were usually small in stature, with bowed legs and thick, flat feet. Their crooked legs were caused by the practice of squatting on their calves. Also, their women wore tight bandages of cloth and beads around their ankles that rendered their legs malformed and swollen.

Their skin tone was the usual copper-brown, and they had fleshy noses and wide mouths with thick lips. Their eyes were generally black, with stringy hair that was also matte black. The men wore animal hides decorated with feathers, and adorned themselves with piercings of bones and sea shells. The woman wore grass-like skirts, with tops made from cedar bark strands. Also, most of the natives wore straw basket hats.

The Tillamooks had no calendar, only a notion of the passing seasons. Indeed, they had only vague concepts of yesterday and tomorrow, and yet they understood the tides almost to the hour. As a people, they were peaceful and seldom went to war. Other nations, however, often raided their lands, killing and stealing. These actions always met with quick and deadly retaliation. When necessary, the Killamucks could be savagely brutal.

For the Tillamooks, each village was the social unit around which life revolved. A typical village was usually an extended clan that had a loosely structured class system in which material wealth was the ruling force.

These villages had four social classes: the leaders, the middle class, the poor and the slaves. The power of the leaders, or chiefs, was limited by the elders and shamans (healers or spirit people). "Chief" was a term used by the white man for any individual who exerted some degree of authority over his people. With the Tillamooks, this title seemed dependent on the task at hand: an expert warrior to lead an attack, an expert fisherman to oversee fishing, or a shrewd trader to deal with other tribes. One village could have many chiefs.

Most people in the villages were middle class. As a group, they wielded

great political power, and had to be consulted before any changes were made that pertained to village life. Below this class were a few poor people who, because of fate or ill health, had been reduced to a lesser social status. These Indians lived in mat houses or abandoned lodges, doing odd jobs such as running errands. The final class was the slave. The typical slave among the Tillamooks could be sold or traded. All slaves lived in the lodges of their owners, and female captives often became wives of their captors. The children of slaves were also slaves, and the custom of killing slaves when the master died was common. Before the white man, the natives had a simple monetary system of small white dentalium shells that were strung together. After contact with white traders, the natives added animal hides as another currency. And, though the Tillamooks were a wealth-oriented society, they also were given to potlatch, a practice of giving gifts to guests, sometimes to the point of poverty for the giver.

The Tillamooks believed that all people experienced three essential periods in their lives: birth, finding their guardian spirit and death. The guardian spirit was the core of their lives; once it was achieved, it would stay with them throughout life and into death. Therefore, the search for this spirit was steeped in tradition and tribal rituals.

These beliefs were so strong that, when the salmon returned to bays and rivers each year, the Indians believed that those fish were the spirits of their dead ancestors. Therefore, they were killed quickly so their souls could be released again and return to the other side. The Tillamooks were true to their faith and had little tolerance for non-believers. If they captured people with a different creed, those individuals were likely killed. Over the centuries, death came easily and often to the Tillamook people, and the tribe developed religious practices and superstitions to deal with the passing of their loved ones. Burials took place four to six days after death. The interim time was allotted for the shamans and relatives to bring the newly deceased person back from the spirit world. Chanting, blood-letting, self-inflicted wounds and fasting all played a part in these ceremonies.

On the sixth day, fasting ended with the eating of fresh fish or game. Then the lodge and all the belongings of the deceased were spiritually purified by the shaman. Sometimes, the death lodge was set ablaze, especially if the person had died of a mysterious disease or because of an evil spirit.

After removing the deceased from the lodge and performing the pre-burial rituals, villagers took the body to a river and cleansed it thoroughly with fresh water, then wrapped it in mats and robes. The personal canoe of the deceased became their crypt, to carry them to the after-life. The inside of the pirogue was painted red, and a hole was drilled in the bottom to release any rainwater that might accumulate. Then the body was placed in an oblong cedar box, and this casket was placed in the canoe, along with the deceased's paddles and personal effects.

Planks were secured over the top of the burial dugout to keep out predators. The canoe was then placed in its final resting spot – in a tree, on a rocky ledge or on the ground. The Octopus Tree at Cape Mears was reserved for only chiefs and shamans. This pirogue placement always faced west and included cedar posts driven into the earth, where the Indians could hang the fishing and eating implements of the deceased, in the belief that these items would be needed for the long journey to the spirit world.

The Octopus Tree at Cape Mears was the final resting place for only chiefs and shamans.

This practice of canoe burials continued until the arrival of white settlers. With the large influx of the whites came the clearing of land, and the pioneers burned most of the burial canoes, partly because of the odor but mostly because they were in the way. Some settlers, needing boats for travel, would dump out the bodies, plug the hole in the bottom, and paddle off. Naturally, this practice was an affront to the Tillamooks, who soon resorted to burying their dead in unmarked graves.

Rare image of a coastal Indian woman named Mary in 1911. At the time of the photo Mary claimed to be 120 years old. Neither her tribe or age could be confirmed.
(Clatsop Historical Society)

The roots of the Tillamook nation grew deep in the sands and surf of the rugged Pacific Northwest coast. The nation's survival is a tribute to a culture of strong men and staunch woman. They were a fiercely proud people who routinely faced and weathered human calamities we can barely imagine.

In 1856, the Tillamooks and twenty other tribes were placed on the Siletz Indian Reservation. At that time, fewer then 200 Tillamook Indians remained. The last full-blooded Tillamook Indian, Ellen Center, died in 1959, at the age of ninety-seven. She had been born in 1862, when the Indians still had one active village on the bay. Her demise marked the end of the great Tillamook nation. †

*This article was condensed from information in a new novel, **Tillamook Passage**, by Brian D. Ratty. For more information on Oregon coastal Indians, the author recommends visiting the Tillamook Pioneer Museum, the Garibaldi Maritime Museum and/or the Clatsop County Historical Society.*

Mickey Mouse

The silver screen flickered to life. Then, over the moaning sound of the projector, came a moving image with a voice.

"Hi, boys and girls. I'm Mickey Mouse, and I'd like to talk to you about polio."

It was 1954 I was in the sixth grade, at Multnomah Grade School, and this was the first time I had ever seen a film produced just for kids. The producer was Walt Disney, the subject was the scourge of polio and a new vaccine developed by Dr. Jonas Salk. It starred Mickey and Goofy, and it was animated, in full color, from start to finish. How fascinating! But I was just as fascinated with the projector that showed the film. When the class asked to see the film again, I asked the teacher if I could watch her reload the projector.

"Sure…and if you stay after class, Brian, I'll teach you how to run the projector."

That's how it all started. That very evening, I told my folks, at the dinner table, that when I grew up I wanted to make films. They smiled and reminded me that I wasn't a very good reader or speller, so what kind of films could I make? They were right, but at age twelve I had already determined my career path!

In the seventh and eighth grades, I was put in charge of all the audio and visual equipment at the school. We had overhead projectors, filmstrip projectors, record players, and two heavy, and awkward, 16mm film projectors, along with screens and carts. The little AV room was full of equipment, and I was the only student to have a key. If a teacher was going to use audio/visuals, I was called in. I would set up, project, remove, and maintain all the AV equipment. I even spun 'platters' (music records) at lunch time and at the 'sock hops.' I guess you can say I was the first 'technical-nerd' in my class.

When I graduated from grade school, all those skills were forgotten. Not until my junior year at Wilson High School, when I took my first photography class, did they return. After graduation, I joined the Oregon Air National Guard as a photo recon photographer. Then, in 1966, I attended, and graduated (1968), from Brooks Institute of Photography. In 1971, my wife and I opened our company, Media West. For over forty years now, we have been producing Audio/Visual programs for industrial and educational markets.

Not bad for a twelve year old…and I owe all to Mickey Mouse! †

Brian D. Ratty

Chapter 2
The Shadow Of Robert Gray

What a crying shame when a person's final days are marked with poverty and thoughts of lost prospects. So it was with Yankee trader Captain Robert Gray. He died at sea at the age fifty-one, near Charleston, South Carolina in 1806. He had reaped no rewards for his years of discovery, and thought himself a failure to the very end. But today Robert Gray's deeds cast a long shadow across the rugged coastline of the Pacific Northwest.

Long before Lewis & Clark trudged across the heartland, Captain Gray was exploring and charting the pristine lands and waterways of the North American Continent. His maiden voyage to the Pacific was a daring enterprise that started in Boston Harbor in October of 1787 and ended in that same harbor on August 1790. During this passage, Captain Gray and his crew of the sloop *Lady Washington* were the first Americans to set foot on the Pacific West Coast when, in August of 1788, they discovered and named Tillamook Bay and the natives who thrived on its shore. Here they traded trinkets with the Indians for sea otter pelts. This they did for many months along the Pacific coastline.

In 1789, now in command of the full-rigged ship *Columbia Rediviva*, he departed Nootka (Vancouver Island) with 1300 prime pelts and sailed for China, via the Sandwich Islands (Hawaii) to trade the skins for Canton tea. When he arrived back in Boston, this black-eye-patched captain became the first American to have circumnavigated the globe. For this accomplishment, he was paraded through Boston and attended a reception held in his honor by Governor John Hancock. While the commercial value of this first voyage was disappointing, due to damaged tea from sea seepage, Captain Gray and the *Columbia* would depart for a second historic voyage to the Northwest in just six short weeks.

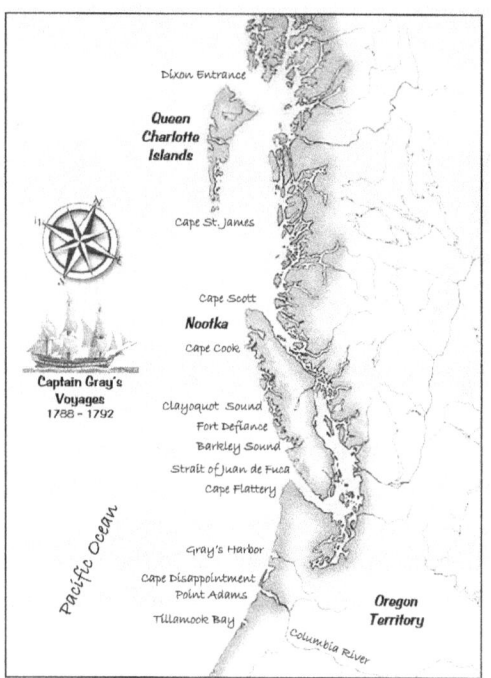

With the *Columbia* overhauled and made ready for sea again, he sailed from Boston Harbor in September 1790. After another long and treacherous trip around Cape Horn, Gray arrived at Clayoquot, an American trading post on Nootka in June of 1791. Here he met up again with the quirky Captain Kendrick and Gray's old ship, the *Lady Washington,* which had been converted from a sloop (single mast) to a brigantine (double mast).

The two ships did not fare well during that summer of discovery. The *Columbia* sailed far north, trading with the natives, but some of his men were murdered by hostile Indians. The *Lady Washington* sailed for the Queen Charlotte Island and was also attacked when a few sailors went ashore. One among those slain was Captain Kendrick's own son.

The two ships returned to the Clayoquot in September, and the *Lady Washington*, under the command of Kendrick, set out for China with the furs from both ships. With winter approaching, Gray and his crew went to work, erecting a log fort which they named Defiance, and building a small 45-ton sloop that he christened *Adventure*. This ship was put under the command of Haswell, Gray's second officer.

The Indians around the tiny American outpost were not friendly, so Gray and his men were obliged to keep constant vigil during the long, dark and wet winter. In early April, both vessels finally departed Clayoquot, with the *Adventure* sailing north for trade and the *Columbia* sailing for the rich sea-otter waters south of Nootka. But Captain Gray was not only searching for furs; he also explored many rivers, bays and inlets that he charted and named.

A few weeks later, after arriving at the southern reaches of the Oregon coast, he turned north again, still seeking safe shelter for his ship and crew. Near the end of April, Gray sighted another ship and hove to for an exchange of greetings with Captain George Vancouver, a British Naval officer commanding the ship *Discovery*. Using a voice-horn, Gray informed the captain that he had recently lain off for nine days at the mouth of a large river where the tides were so violent that he dared not attempt to cross the bar. Vancouver doubted this news but noted in his journal: "If any river should be found, it must be a very intricate one and inaccessible to vessels of our burden." The *Discovery* pushed on northward.

Gray continued on his journey, trading along the way. As he sailed up the coastline, the lookouts kept a keen eye out for any safe harbor in which the *Columbia* could lay over. On May 7th, Gray noted in his log book the discovery of what would become known as Grays Harbor: "Being within six miles of the land, saw an entrance in the same… We soon saw from our masthead a passage in between the sand-bars…as we drew in nearer between the bars, had from ten to thirteen fathoms, having a very strong tide of ebb to stem… in a safe harbor, well sheltered from sea by long bars and spits."

After spending but a short time in the harbor he had just discovered, Gray decided to sail south again to enter the mouth of the river he had sighted. This time luck and the tides were with him. A small yawl was launched to locate a safe passage across the treacherous bar which flowed with the strong, muddy current of a great river. According to the ship's log, the crossing was made on May 11, 1792. Gray recorded the historic event: "At eight a.m. being a little to windward of the entrance of the harbor, bore away, and run in east-north-east between the breakers… When we were over the bar, we found this to be a large river of fresh water, up we steered… The north side of the river a half mile distant from the ship; the south side of the same two and a half miles distance… Vast numbers of natives came alongside… pumping the salt water out of our watercasks, in order to fill with fresh, while ship floated in. So ends."

The ship Columbia Rediviva Underway

Gray had found the "Great River of the West" and yet described the event with one of history's most understated comments: "So ends." It is almost as if he considered this discovery unimportant. The *Columbia* sailed upriver, trading nails and other trinkets to the Indians for pelts, salmon, and animal meat. During this nine-day journey, Gray named many landmarks, bays and inlets. He also named the mighty river 'Columbia,' after his ship; the cape to the south bar became 'Adams,' and the one to the north, 'Hancock' (now referred to as Cape Disappointment). While on the river, Gray made a detailed chart of his discoveries, a copy of which was later acquired by Captain Vancouver.

Captain Gray sailed to China in 1793 and sold his furs. The venture must have not been profitable as he was not sent out to repeat it. Captain Kendrick of the *Lady Washington* was killed in the Sandwich Islands in a cannon accident in 1794. Gray's many discoveries apparently impressed the public little more than they had impressed Gray himself, for he never sailed the far Pacific again. Neither recognition nor wealth befell him. Impoverished, he died in 1806 of yellow fever.

Gray did not publish his discoveries concerning the Columbia River, nor those elsewhere along the far reaches of the Pacific coast. But Captain Vancouver did, giving Gray full credit for the many years he spent plying the waters of the Northwest. At the time, these discoveries by Gray were considered unimportant. However, other Americans soon followed up on the trading opportunities pioneered by Gray, who were called "Boston man" by the local Indians. By 1801, sixteen American vessels were engaged in the fur trade and the triangular route to China. Moreover, Gray's discovery of the Columbia River was later used by the United States Government in support of its territorial claims to what Americans called the Oregon Country.

Today, Captain Gray's shadow is more like a rainbow across the vast Pacific Northwest. Many namesakes for this famous explorer, Yankee trader and sea captain can be found on maps and nautical charts: harbors, bays, rivers, inlets and other geographic points are named for him. In addition, one Washington State county, a small village, a few avenues, and many schools bear his name. Captain Robert Gray may have died in obscurity, but his memory as a man with true grit and vision lives on. †

*This article was condensed from information in a new novel, **Tillamook Passage**, by Brian D. Ratty. For more information on Captain Robert Gray, the author recommends visiting the Garibaldi Maritime Museum and/or your local library.*

Paperboy

After I turned twelve years old, my father announced one evening that I was old enough to get my first job. He suggested I get an evening paper route. My mother thought the idea was horrible, as I was too young and immature. I eagerly agreed with father, and promised mother that I would be more dependable. She had heard my lame promises before, and just rolled her eyes. But after a few more evenings of prompting and promises, she reluctantly relented and agreed to the idea.

A few weeks later, I got my neighborhood paper route and was excited to have my first job. The route was small, only about forty homes, all scattered close to where my family lived. I picked up my papers at a drop box at four o'clock in the afternoon and finished the route two hours later. My last customer lived next to a drive-in restaurant, where I often rewarded myself with a cherry coke and a piece of pie.

For years, I trudged that route in all weather conditions, seven days a week, on my bike and on foot. That first job taught me many things: dependability, responsibility, customer service, and salesmanship. But I did have one big problem: collections. In those days, the paperboy collected the monthly paper bill. I hated that part of the job, having to spend my weekends ringing doorbells with my hand out. This problem of collecting money would haunt me throughout my early career. Ugh!

When I turned fourteen, I changed newspapers and got a morning route that was twice the size of my old evening route. My papers were delivered to the drop box at 4AM and, with my canvas bag of papers over my shoulders and a flashlight in hand, I started the three-hour route at 5AM and finished just in time for school. I don't recall my parents ever being worried that I was roaming the neighborhood streets all alone at that hour of the day. It was just a different time and place, back then.

This bigger route helped hone my door-to-door salesman skills, and when I was fifteen, I won a city-wide sales contest and a trip to newly opened Disneyland in California. This was a big deal for us paperboys! There was lots of news about the contest and the boys that won. Having won the trip, I announced that I was sending an invitation to famous movie star and pin-up girl, Marilyn Monroe, for a date. My story made the paper and planted dreams in my head about me and Miss Monroe together in Tinseltown. She never did answer my letter… Gee, I wonder why? But I did learn that being a smart salesman was a good thing! †

Chapter 3
Fortress Astoria

Vancouver Shipyard 1943

As a young boy living on the north coast in the early 1940's, I had many heroes. There were Tom Mix and Gene Autry, of course, but my biggest heroes were the tall, handsome Navy pilots that I saw working with my father at the Astoria Airport. That's what I wanted to be: a pilot. A Navy pilot.

Astoria, Oregon, played a pivotal role in helping America win World War II. This sleepy little fishing and logging community on the Columbia River helped to provide a fleet of 455 ships to the war effort.

Shortly before America entered the war, in 1940, a man by the name of Henry J. Kaiser secured a contract to build 31 cargo ships for the British Government. The Brits were in a bad way, standing alone as they fought the Nazis in Europe. They needed help, and the American Government was beginning to provide them with some much-needed war materials.

Kaiser was a genius of a man, with a worldwide reputation as a can-do industrialist. He had recently completed the Hoover Dam, finishing the project in half the time and under budget. If you needed something BIG done, Kaiser was your man.

With the British contract in hand, Kaiser searched the coastal communities for the best locations to build his shipyards. The sites had to be on a navigable waterway, with a large local workforce and a good transportation system. In addition, the locations had to have access to cheap energy, as his shipyards would run twenty-four hours a day. His first selection was ninety miles upstream from Astoria, on the shores of the Columbia River, next to Portland, Oregon. This area offered low-priced hydro power and had a large population nearby, with excellent railroad connections.

As the shipyard was being built, Kaiser and his nautical engineers designed the first Liberty ship. Their concept was simple: make the ships durable, inexpensive and easy to build. During the course of WWII, eighteen American shipyards would build 2,710 Liberty ships using the Kaiser design. On May 19, 1941, Kaiser's Oregon Shipbuilding Corporation launched the very first Liberty ship, *The Star of Oregon*. However, of the first five ships built that year, all were sunk in action within months of their commissioning. England was losing the war!

After the surprise attack by the Japanese on Pearl Harbor on December 7, 1941, America entered WWII. As Kaiser constructed another shipyard, across the river in Vancouver, Washington, he and his engineers designed a new type of aircraft carrier that would become known as the Casablanca-class Escort Carrier. The 'baby-flattops' would be built using the standard hull of the Liberty ship, with a flight deck on top. These small carriers would be used for convoy duty and to resupply the larger fleet aircraft carriers with planes and crews. The concept was again simple and easy to build. Within months of finishing the plans, Kaiser had a U.S. Navy contract to build fifty ships. During the war, Kaiser also expanded his operations in Oregon and started building Liberty ships and T2 tankers for the U.S. Maritime Commission.

USS Coral Sea
CVE-57 1943

ircraft carriers need planes and crews, and that's where Astoria came in. The
Navy already had a Naval Air Station (NAS) on Tongue Point, just east of the
town, where PBY Catalina seaplanes arrived for coastal patrols. In addition, Astoria had a
good-sized municipal airport with room to grow, and the Navy liked the towns deep-
water location, so near to the mouth of the Columbia River. Best of all, this entire estuary
was protected by the 249th Coast Artillery. Fort Columbia stood on the north side of the
river, with Fort Stevens on the south shore. These units also maintained and mined the
mouth of the Columbia River. This 'iron triangle' of defense made Astoria a formidable
fortress.

My Grandfather Harry had worked for years for the U.S. Navy, maintaining
lighthouses up and down the coast. In 1940, he became the head of civilian construction
at Tongue Point NAS. He and his crews built barracks, chow halls, shops, movie theaters
and administrative buildings. Prior to the start of the war, my father, Dudley Ratty, did
the same kind of work for the Army in Alaska. Early in 1941, with the war looming, all
non-essential civilians were ordered back to the lower-forty eight. This meant a long,
lonely ship ride for my mother Evelyn and older sister Diane. After the war started,
grandfather got dad a job with the Navy as a civilian carpenter. He soon became the head
of civilian construction for Astoria Naval Air Station.

The primary mission of the Astoria NAS was to train Navy pilots and crews on the
new types of combat planes that would serve on Escort Carriers. They would also instruct
the pilots on short-field landings and take-offs, in preparation for the small decks of the
baby-flattops. Additionally, the Navy had training schools for aircraft maintenance, radio

operation, a naval hospital, a receiving station and many other U.S. Navy offices at the airfield. The runways were lengthened, new ones were added, and hangars were built to handle the flood of arriving aircraft. Astoria NAS was a fast-growing city with its own police force, chow halls, barracks and movie theaters.

New planes arrived every day from manufacturers up and down the West Coast. Each Escort Carrier required a minimum of twenty-eight planes. Soon, the gray skies around the airfield filled with all types of aircraft: Grumman F4F Wildcat fighters, the Avenger torpedo bombers, the Douglas SBD dive bombers, C47 cargo planes and, from Tongue Point, the Catalina flyboats. As the pilots and crews trained, there were many accidents. Some planes went down during their training flights, while others crashed upon landing or, as my father told me years later, some pilots undershot the runway and ditched in the shallow, muddy waters of Young's Bay. This was a dangerous business, with young, inexperienced pilots at the controls.

On the home front, the tiny Astoria rail station filled with strange faces and voices from all around America. These men and woman had different accents, uniforms and life styles. They filled the quiet streets, bars, shops and waterfront, turning Astoria into a more diverse crab-pot. There was rationing of everything: food, gas, rubber and scrap metal. And as the local men marched off to war, the local women stepped forward, taking over their jobs. There were women fishermen, lumber jacks, bartenders and auto mechanics. While Portland had 'Rosie, the Riveter,' Astoria boasted the amazing and resourceful 'Daughters of the Columbia.' Everyone pulled together for one common cause – the war effort.

After the Escort Carriers were completed in Vancouver, they steamed to Astoria for sea-trials across the Columbia Bar. If the carrier performed to the high standards set by the many Navy supervisors aboard, the ship would be commissioned into the fleet. Once this was accomplished, the carrier sailed again for the open ocean and waited for her aircraft and flight crews to arrive from the Astoria NAS. This marrying of ship and planes on the open sea was another very dangerous time for the untested pilots. Some had trouble landing on the small, twisting flight deck, while others over-shot the deck and crashed into the cold sea. Carrier pilots had to have nerves of steel. Finally, with all the planes recovered, the Escort Carrier, with a complement of just over nine hundred officers and men, would steam towards their first combat assignment.

In less than two years, Kaiser built and delivered all fifty carriers to the Navy. At the end of the war, America had lost twelve aircraft carriers to enemy action. Five of those sunk were Casablanca-class Escort Carriers, built on the Columbia River.

VJ-Day August 15, 1945

I never became a Navy pilot, but I served in the Oregon Air National Guard And, with the anniversary of the end of WWII approaching (August 15), I realize that my early heroes should have included ALL of the men and woman, in or out of uniform, who helped defeat the tyranny of our enemies. *As we pay tribute to the WWII generation, let us never forget that we share our tomorrows because of their yesterdays!* †

What's In A Name?

At fifteen years old, I secured my first real job, pumping gas at a local Standard Oil station. There I was taught to always thank my customers by using the last name on their credit card.

One day, while finishing up with a patron, I said "Thank you, Mr. Soe."

The customer left, giving me a puzzled look. My boss, who overheard this transaction, said "Mr. Soe? That's a funny name."

I replied, "What's funnier, this is the third Mr. Soe I've helped this week!"

Reaching for the receipt, my boss rolled his eyes. "The last letters on his credit card, SOE, means 'Standard Oil Employee, you dummy!"

A few nights later, I had another problem. After looking at a patrons name on his credit card, I couldn't bring myself to say it out loud.

Instead I stammered, "Thank you, Mr. Fllll."

The man looked at me with disdain. "It's FLUCK, son, F.L.U.C.K. Don't forget it!"

After that night, I stopped reading customer names, and called everyone sir or ma'am! †

Chapter 4
Rescue From The Rock

Tillamook Rock Lighthouse 1934

With trees snapping and winds howling in the many disastrous coastal winter storms, my mind raced back to my Grandfather, Harry, and his daring rescue off the Tillamook Rock Lighthouse in 1934.

As a young boy in the early 1950's, I remember visiting my grandparent's home in west Portland where, over the fireplace mantel, hung two black and white photographs that Harry had neatly framed. These images, which had appeared in the National Geographic Magazine in August of 1936, helped him tell his story of being rescued from the Rock. After his death in 1970, those photos and his story became just a foggy memory to me. Then, last year, a cousin loaned me a tattered box full of family memorabilia. Deep inside, I found both the yellowing photographs and my grandfather's story on faded newspaper clippings. With the aid of today's technology, I was able to restore both the images and the story of his daring rescue.

In the 1930's, Harry Ratty worked for the Lighthouse Service as a maintenance engineer. He traveled from Cape Disappointment to Coos Bay, repairing the many lighthouses that dotted the region. These bright white sentinels were manned 24-7 by keepers who spent months on station. Harry and his crews kept their lights burning, the fog horns blasting, and the keepers safe from the terrible elements.

My grandfather was a quiet man with that Oregon spirit of rugged independence. Just after the turn of the century, he entered the building trades and helped shape the Portland skyline with structures like the J.K. Gill Building, the Lipman Wolfe Building and the old Multnomah Hotel. In 1928, he helped build the Big Dipper roller coaster at the Jantzen Beach Amusement Park. Coincidentally, my father Dudley (also a contractor) tore down that same coaster in 1972. Harry also worked on the Bonneville Dam and, during World War II, was in charge of the civilian contractors at the Warrenton Naval Air Station on the north coast. But, of all of his accomplishments, it was the Rock that he talked about the most.

Harry Ratty right front (Age 48) 1934 on Tillamook Rock
Lighthouse. Note sandbags on left stacked against the wall.

Tillamook Rock Lighthouse, also known as Terrible Tillie, is the most exposed lighthouse on the Pacific coast, and has survived many violent storms. Although the lantern is 133 feet above the level of the sea, the protective glass has, on more than one occasion, been shattered by stones hurled by giant waves. In 1878, Congress appropriated $50,000 for the construction of a lighthouse on the crest of Tillamook Rock, a huge stone monolith just over a mile west of Tillamook Head and twenty miles south of the Columbia River entrance. It took nearly three years for the Army Corps of Engineers to chisel out the lighthouse. During the building of the station, a lighthouse engineer lost his life while attempting a landing on the Rock.

In October of 1934, a violent storm swept over the Rock, causing over $5,000 damage to lighthouse. As the storm finally retreated, Harry and his crew were landed on the Rock via lighthouse tender. A few weeks later, while extensive repairs were being made, a second ferocious storm blew up from the south. This one had winds of over 75 mph and sent 60-pound boulders smashing against the light tower and stone building. Power was lost again, as was the telephone cable to shore. With windows broken, rain and sea pouring in, and the light's Fresnel lens shattered, the four marooned keepers and five-man work party rode out the gale for almost five days. Finally, one of the keepers, a ham radio operator, made contact with shore for rescue. During this time Harry, a crew member and one of the other keepers were taken seriously ill as a result of exposure. A rescue boat was sent but, after two days of unsuccessful attempts to remove them from the Rock, the lighthouse tender Rose was dispatched. In dangerous, stormy waters, she was able to shoot a rope line to the lighthouse and rig up a breeches buoy from the Rock to her deck. Riding the breeches buoy from the lighthouse, over the churning waters, to the pitching deck of the Rose was an experience my grandfather would never forget. By the time Harry (pictured) reached the tender, riding just over the bobbing safety boat, his shoes were wet and his nerves frayed. Aboard the tender was a Coast Guard photographer, who took the pictures. Harry and four others were removed from the lighthouse in this manner while replacement crews and supplies were sent back up. My grandfather and two of the others were sent on to Astoria for medical treatment.

Harry Ratty riding the breeches buoy

This story of rescue was national news and made the front pages of many newspapers. The box of clippings and family memorabilia brings new meaning to Grandfather Harry's recollections and the importance of struggling through any 'storm.' Digging deeper into this box, I also found a tattered copy of a Western Union telegram addressed to Harry while he was recovering at the Astoria Hospital. It was a message from his wife, Elsie, (my grandmother), still back in Portland. It simply read: Glad you are well –stop- Come home soon -stop- Bills need to be paid –stop.

So much for Harry's fifteen seconds of fame and his rescue from the Rock! In 1957 the lighthouse was decommissioned and the island sold. †

Party Room Prank

The apple didn't fall far from my father's tree. We both had a good sense of humor and enjoyed playing pranks whenever possible. This one happened when I was only twelve.

For Christmas of 1954, my parents gave me a portable record player with removable speakers and a microphone, so I could sing along. This was really a bad idea, as I couldn't carry a tune in a wheel barrow. But I did enjoy listening to hits of the day, like *Mr. Sandman,* and *Rock Around the Clock* by Bill Haley And The Comets.

My mother had found the plans for our family home in a movie magazine. It was a large, ranch-style house, with a round living room and a full basement. The cellar was a big L-shaped room which housed the laundry, furnace and canning storage. As a youth of twelve, I found the basement, with its dark corners, rattling pipes and glowing oil furnace, to be both scary and inviting. But the largest downstairs area was the party room, complete with fireplace, wet bar, phonograph, and overstuffed furniture resting on a vinyl floor. Here, mother and father held many parties for a group of old friends they called 'the gang.'

As was their tradition, they hosted a New Year's Eve party for the gang, that year. Before their guests arrived, my father borrowed my portable record player and placed one of the speakers under the upstairs toilet, closest to the party room. After helping him hide the speaker wire, I showed him how to use the microphone, which he then hid downstairs with the phonograph. I had no idea what he was planning.

When the guests arrived, the party started. As usual, my sister and I remained up in the living room, watching television, but we could hear the party music and laughter from below us. A few hours later, we heard a blood-curdling scream from the upstairs bathroom! Rushing to the hallway, we found Helen H, an old friend and good-natured, big woman, standing outside the bathroom, trying to pull up her girdle.

She was screaming at the top of lungs for my father. "Dudley? Dudley! Someone is under your house!"

"What happened?" I asked, trying to calm her down.

She looked at me with a puzzled expression. "I'd no more than sat down on the toilet when a strange man's voice shouted up to me, "Pardon me, ma'am, we're working down here. Can you please move over?" †

Chapter 5
Mountain Men

T here would be no Mountain Men without the fur trade. This enterprise was driven by the fashions of the time. Euro-Americans demanded hats made of beaver skins and coats made of buffalo hides. In China and Europe, there was a great clamor for otter pelts and other skins. To answer these calls, powerful fur companies were formed. The British controlled the Hudson Bay Company, the French dominated the North West Company and John Astor monopolized the American Fur Company and later the Pacific Fur Company. These companies, and the many other smaller regional fur outfits, would flourish economically for the first half of the nineteenth century.

There were essentially three realms of business: the Maritime trade, the Rocky Mountain trade and the Upper Missouri fur trade. All these regions had particular circumstances and hence very different methods of operating. The Maritime trade operated primarily on the Pacific Coast, and required shiploads of goods, as well as fearless sailors to trade with the many different Indian Nations. In this realm, the most desired pelts were otter and beaver, which were killed and cured by the local Indians.

The Upper Missouri trade relied on the Indian tribes to bring their buffalo skins to trading posts and forts. There, the robes were sold and then sent to St. Louis, via river.

The Rocky Mountain realm was quite different, and beaver was the fur of choice. The beaver were trapped mainly by Canadian and American Mountain Men traveling in large troops. The hides were sold at a yearly rendezvous, with the buyers traveling overland to the designated site and then hauling out the furs via mule train or wagon train to be sold in the cities. This system allowed the Mountain Men to stay in the wilderness year-round, as they did not have to travel to a trading post to sell their pelts.

The Mountain Man was a slave to the fur market created by the competing fur companies. In a good year, a beaver pelt could be worth ten dollars; in a bad year, it brought only half that amount. The control a company had over a trapper depended on his contract. 'Engages' were men who were supplied and salaried by the company. The furs they collected were the property of the company. 'Skin Trappers' were outfitted by the company in exchange for a set share of their pelts at the end of the season. The 'Free-Trapper' was at the top of this social pyramid, and was beholden to no company. He outfitted himself and trapped wherever and with whomever he pleased. Contrary to the common belief of lone trappers plying the waters for beaver, the Mountain Men usually traveled in brigades of forty to sixty men, including camp tenders, meat hunters, scouts and interpreters. From base camps, they would fan out and trap in parties of two or three. It was then that the trappers were most vulnerable to Indian attack. Indians were a constant threat, and confrontation was common. Once the beaver were trapped, they were skinned immediately; the pelts were allowed to dry, and then were folded in half, fur to the inside. Unlike buffalo skins, beaver pelts were compact, light and portable.

The Mountain Man's life was not ruled by the calendar or clock, but by the climate and seasons. The legends and feats of famous Mountain Men such as Jedediah Smith, Jim Bridger and Christopher (Kit) Carson, to name but a few, have survived the test of time because there was truth to the tales they told. The life of the Mountain Man was rough, and brought him face to face with death on a regular basis; sometimes through the slow agony of starvation, dehydration, burning heat, or freezing cold and sometimes by the surprise attack of animal or Indian. But the rewards for these hardships could also be bright. Jedediah Smith came out of the wilderness in eleven years with a half-million-dollar fortune, in today's money. The lucrative earnings of the fur trade helped propel John Astor to his status as America's richest man. Joe Meek, a famous trapper and early pioneer in the Oregon Country, once wrote of the Mountain Men: "…They prided themselves on their hardihood and courage, even on their recklessness and profligacy. Each claimed to own the best horse; to have had the wildest adventure; to have made the narrowest escapes; to have killed the greatest number of bears and Indians; to be the greatest favorite with the Indian belles, the greatest consumer of alcohol, and to have the most money to spend…" It is estimated that over one thousand Mountain Men roamed the American West from 1820 to 1840, the heyday of the fur trade. †

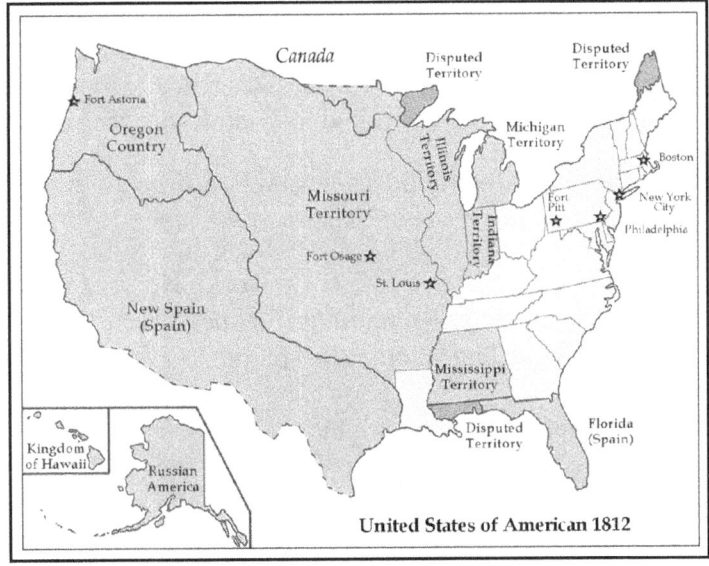

This article was condensed from information in a new novel, **Destination Astoria**, by Brian D. Ratty. For more information on Mountain Men, the author recommends the books: **Across the Wide Missouri** by Bernard Devoto, **The River of the West** by Frances Fuller Victor, and **Trask** by Don Berry.

Jock

Father Dudley, myself, Sister Diane & Mother Evelyne

I grew up in a working-class family, my parents struggled to give my sister and me the best they could afford. This meant that mom and dad went without, for many years. In the early 1950's, when I was seven or eight years old, my folks finally had saved enough money to buy a brand-new red Ford pickup truck for my dad. They were so proud of this vehicle that we often drove around town in it, not the older family car.

During this time, one of my boyhood friends was a neighborhood kid named Jock. He and I were inseparable, making mischief wherever we went.

One morning, my father went out to go to work. He froze in his tracks as he approached his new truck, then started screaming for me. When I joined him outside on the driveway, he was red-faced and about to explode. Someone had scratched Jock's name on his driver-side door!

"Did you do this?" he asked, calmly with his fists clenched.

"No, Father," I answered with my most honest face. "Jock did."

He glared at me for longest time. "You lie," he finally said, fuming. "Jock knows how to spell his own name, while obviously you don't. That's why YOU scratched JOK in my damn door!"

He flashed me one of his 'looks,' and fear filled my heart. He had me dead to rights. I had done the deed, and we both knew that I was the worst speller in my class. I can't remember what happened next; I must have run like hell! †

Looking back on my childhood, I often wonder how I lived through those mischievous years of my life…Only by the grace of God, and loving parents.

Chapter 6
Give 'em Hell, Harry

Recently, sixty-five nationally acclaimed historians came out with their annual ratings for America's best presidents. Abraham Lincoln topped the list again, followed by George Washington, Franklin D. Roosevelt, Theodore Roosevelt and Harry S. Truman. If you had a chance to sit down and talk to one of these great men, what would you say? What would you ask? Well, I had just such an opportunity, and here's my story.

In the spring of 1961, having just been detached from active duty with the US Air Force, I was traveling home to Portland, Oregon, from Denver, Colorado. The United Airlines flight that I boarded, that fine spring day, had originated in Chicago, with stops at Denver, Portland, and the final destination, Seattle.

Moving up the outside boarding ladder, dressed in my blue Airman 2nd Class uniform, I entered the DC-8 jetliner through the center fuselage door. As I made my way down the center aisle, I found the plane about half full, and began looking for my assigned seat. As luck would have it, I found my window seat just over one of the wings, next to a young sailor who was also in uniform. As the aircraft prepared for takeoff, the Navy guy and I made small talk, and boy, did we have a lot to talk about: John F. Kennedy had been sworn in as the 35th President (1961-1963), just a few months before. Already, our country had witnessed the dismal failure of the Bay of Pigs invasion in Cuba, and had faced down Russia in the Cuban Missile Crisis. These were hot topics for two servicemen, at the time.

As the plane reached its cruising altitude, I began noticing an unusual number of coach passengers passing through the draped doorway to the forward First Class compartment, each returning a few moments later.

Turning to the sailor, I asked, "What's all the action, up front?"

"Harry Truman is up there. He got on in Chicago."

"We should go shake his hand," I replied.

With a scowl he answered, "I wouldn't walk across the aisle for that SOB!"

Harry entertaining with Lauren Bacall

1949 Political Cartoon

Former President, Harry S. Truman, (1945-1953), had finished his term little more than eight years before, at the low ebb of his popularity. He had been blamed for many things…but, in the end, he had been proven right about almost everything. This was the President who had a plaque on his Oval Office desk that read 'The Buck Stops Here,' and he was known for his 'Give 'em Hell' attitude. I had always liked him!

"Well, I'm going to shake his hand. Never met a President before. You sure you won't come?"

Pushing his Dixie-cup hat lower down his forehead, the sailor shook his head no.

I was nervous as I approached the draped doorway, but being in uniform gave me solace. Pulling the cloth back, I found a small First Class compartment with a pair of double seats facing each other on both sides. There were only two men in the entire compartment. On my right, facing me, was a large fellow dressed in a business suit, staring at my every move. He had to be Secret Service. On my left, also facing me, was the former President of the United States. I was overwhelmed with pride and scared to death! His face looked older and more tired than I remembered it from his photographs. With my hand outstretched, I took a few steps and simply said, "Mr. President I, would like to shake your hand."

When he looked up from the magazine he was reading, a broad, warm smile raced across his face. Extending his hand, he replied, "Airman, I would like to shake yours."

His handshake was firm and solid for a seventy-seven year old man. Nodding towards the empty seat in front of him, he continued, "Sit down, Airman. Let's talk."

It took a second for my knees to stop shaking and start bending. Sitting down on the edge of the seat in front of him, I asked, "Mr. President, where are you going today?"

With his blue eyes peering into my soul, he answered, "Have to make a speech up in Seattle, but that's not important. Where are *you* going, Airman?"

That's how it started. I asked him another four or five simple questions. He answered all my queries but always turned the conversation back to me. "Where you from, son?...Do you like the Air Force?...What do you do in the Air Force?...Are you married or have a girlfriend?" Always the conversation came back to me! But it was more than that: it was the way he looked at me, as if I were the most important person on the plane. It was also his eyes, bright and alert, always seeming to pierce through to my soul.

I would like to say we talked for half an hour, but I'm sure it was only a few minutes. When I finally got my legs to work again, and stood up to leave, he shook my hand again.

"Nice talking to you, Airman. God bless you."

Looking into his steel-blue eyes for the last time, I knew I was in the presence of a great leader, as well as a famous President.

Upset: Harry Wins!

The Buck Stops Here

Walking back to my seat, I couldn't believe how fortunate I had been to meet the former President of the United States. I knew I would remember that brief encounter for the rest of my life, and here I am, writing about it almost fifty years later! Therefore, I was not surprised by the historians recent decision to name Harry S. Truman as one of this nation's greatest Presidents. He was, and I had the honor to meet him! †

Dream And A Truck

In 1962, fresh out of active duty with the Air Force, I started a new career as a milkman! Yes... do you remember that era? My young bride at the time told all of her friends that I worked in the 'dairy industry'... guess she was embarrassed with my new position. But it was a Union job and I made *really* good money. Carnation dairy had over fifty retail routes in the Portland metro area. My long and demanding route served over six hundred customers in Vancouver Washington. My day started at 4:30 AM and wasn't over until late in the afternoon when I completed my daily accounting in the route room. Shagging milk in all kinds of weather, at all hours was a tough job!

Sometimes we drivers would go to the evening Teamsters meetings (The Union *we* paid BIG dues to) and ask questions about our retirement fund. Jimmy Hoffa was the Union president at the time, but he was in jail. The rumors were that the Union was skimming off the top of our retirement fund to pay off his lawyers. We'd ask questions about this, and were promptly tossed out of the hall. I went to a few of these meetings and then stopped going. Never did see a penny from my retirement fund!

But being a milkman changed my life forever... here's how: I had just started my forth year at the dairy. It was one COLD miserable day with snow, rain and sleet. Late that afternoon, I stumbled up the stairs to the route room hours late. The work tables were packed with other wet and tired drivers. As I did my bookkeeping I noticed an older milkman across from me. He looked like I felt, and that's when it hit me! He'd been on his route for almost twenty years, making the same money as me, running and lifting just like me, being exhausted just like me... was this my future?

Driving home that evening in my 1952 F-100 Ford pickup, I had an epiphany. I would quit Carnation and go to the school of my dreams! Finally my future was bright and my path clear. Later that night, I told my young wife of my decision and she looked at me with startled expression. Her only words, "If you think I'm putting you through collage, you're dreaming!"

Within the week, my pickup was packed, and I was on my way to Santa Barbara, California and Brooks Institute of Photography. Now after forty years in the media business my only regret is selling that pickup... I sure loved that old truck! †

Chapter 7
California Dreaming

With the song California Dreamin' blaring on the radio, I sped my black 1962 Ford Fairlane and U-Haul trailer south, down Highway 101, towards Santa Barbara California. It was spring time '66, and with the vast blue Pacific Ocean on my right, I was finally heading for my dream destination, Brooks Institute of Photography. At age twenty-four, I had escaped a turbulent marriage and years of being a milkman. My dream of becoming a professional photographer was before me, and I was determined to make my mark on the industry I loved. Who knew, maybe I'd become a great film director or a famous cameraman. The future was mine! And as the song lyrics said, 'I'd be safe and warm…with California dreamin'.

Brooks students shooting a car ad

The campus of the school was tucked into the hills of Montecito, a wealthy community just south of Santa Barbara, overlooking the ocean. The small private school estate had been previously built and owned by Henry Ford. The student body was about two hundred students, with a new class starting every four months. My class started with eighteen students; twenty-eight months later, only six of our original class would graduate. The school had strict rules: no beards, no long hair, no smoking pot, no talking back, and you had to wear a white shirt to class. If you violated those rules, you were out! And many other students who weren't kicked out or *dropped* out, quite due to high tuition costs. Brooks was a highly selective school with an excellent reputation.

Because of the high cost of living in Santa Barbara, many of the students lived in a small art community just south of Montecito, called Summerland. Here, a rag-tag bunch of hippies, surfers, artists and photographers lived in the hills overlooking Highway 101 and the ocean beyond. The little town was quite picturesque, filled with California dreamers of all types. I rented a small apartment with a swimming pool, and promptly dyed my hair blonde and worked on my tan. I even started thinking about buying a surfboard. But I kept reminding myself that I couldn't afford to join the 'endless summer' bunch. A few months later, another classmate and I moved into a triplex with a two-bedroom apartment.

My school classmates varied in talent and temperament, and it wasn't long before a few exceptional students stood out. One was John P, a gifted fine artist by vocation. He painted mostly oil color nudes, and galleries showed his work in Kansas City, Palm Springs, and Hollywood. He hoped to combine his art and photography into a new type of media. His wife's name was Carol, a beautiful woman who worked as a professional model. Over time, John and I became friends and shared many cups of coffee together. He was Polish, and had a fiery personality. One Saturday night, just after I moved into the triplex, I was invited to dinner. They lived just few buildings down from me; if I stood on my balcony, I could look right into their living room. With the sun low on the horizon, I walked to their home that evening, thinking about how I was flourishing in this little art community. Dinner with a famous artist and his beautiful wife and model – if only the other milkmen in the old route room could see me now!

One of Johns paintings

Johns Wife Carol

I arrived on time and was given a short tour of their modern two-story apartment. It was impressive. The stairway was lined with many of John's fine art paintings. And everywhere you looked, there were photos of Carol on her different photo assignments. Wine was served as the three of us stood looking at John's art.

"See anything similar in John's nudes?" Carol asked.

I looked more closely. They were all of beautiful women; blondes, redheads and brunettes, all posed in classic Playboy styles. "No, other than John's talent for painting," I answered.

Carol smiled. "They all have my body. John poses me in his studio, and then adds different faces and skin tones. It cuts down on the model fees."

I'll be damned if she wasn't right. Each did look the same, right down to a small butterfly tattoo on the upper thigh. But staring at paintings of her naked body while she stood next to me was a little embarrassing, so I turned away.

Their kitchen had a small eating bar, where John and I sat on the living room side while, across from us, Carol sat on the kitchen side. She lit a few candles and then served a Caesar salad with more wine. With the sun setting, the conversation was light and friendly. But then something happened, and they started to scream at each other. I can't remember why; all I knew was they were having one hell of an argument. At one point, Carol hurled her bowl of salad at John. With romaine lettuce all over his face, he punched her across the bar so hard that she fell to the kitchen floor with a thud. John jumped to his feet, calling her every name in the book, and rushed to the other side of the bar. She looked up from the floor, with a trickle of blood coming from her nose, and calmly said, "Oh sweetie, how I love you." I was stunned. All this happened while I sat frozen in place, with a heaping portion of salad on my fork, not believing my eyes and ears. Then John reached down, picked her up into his arms, and walked to the stairs.

Turning to me, he said nonchalantly, "We will make love now. Please don't leave. Have some more wine and enjoy the sunset. We will be back down shortly."

And that's what I did. Sometime later, they came downstairs and we had a wonderful meal, as if nothing had happened. As I was leaving that night, Carol said to me, "I know you can see into our apartment from your balcony. I vacuum every Saturday morning in the nude. I thought you might like to know that."

Wow, I was confused. While walking back to my apartment that night, I felt like a priest caught in a lingerie store. Life was so much simpler back on the milk route...*Maybe I wasn't ready for California Dreamin'.* †

 # Dr. D. Bumstead

In the early spring of 1968, I patiently waited for graduation from Brooks Institute of Photography in Santa Barbara, California. At twenty-six years old, I looked forward to starting a new career in photography. But, just before the celebration, I was brought to my knees with pain from deep inside my jaw. There was something desperately wrong with a tooth, and I had to find some relief. Dentists have never been my favorite people, but the magnitude of my anguish soon drove to me to the local yellow pages. Under 'Dentist and Oral Surgeons' I found a listing for a doctor in town. The phone was quickly in my hand as I called a Dr. D. Bumstead to make an appointment for that very afternoon.

At the time, I didn't give a thought to this doctor's name. Maybe it was all that pain, or maybe I had other things on my mind. In any event, his name didn't set off any alarms. (For those who might not know, there was a Dagwood Bumstead in the funny papers. This character has been on television, on radio, and in the comic strips for years. He was the type of fellow that always got into jams and then bungled his way out of them.) But, by the time I walked into this doctor's office, my mind had not made that connection.

On one side of the small room was a glass window, with a chrome desk bell and a sign that said 'check-in.' When I rang the bell, a blonde-haired nurse soon appeared on the other side of the glass, clipboard in hand. With my jaw throbbing, I soon had my registration form filled out and handed back to the nurse.

"Have a seat," she said, smiling. "I'll call you when the doctor is available."

Taking a seat in the vacant waiting room, I prayed for relief, and wondered at the blank, bleak walls, there weren't even stacks of magazines on the empty tables. A few minutes later, the door next to the window opened, and out walked the same nurse.

She gazed upon the empty room, moving her head left and right, and then shouted, "Brian Ratty… Is Brian Ratty here?"

Slowly, I stood, with a queer look on my painful face as she repeated this strange shout for a second time.

Soon, I was seated in a dentist chair in a small examining room. From where I rested, I could look down a short hall and see another small room at the other end, with an empty chair. On both sides of this hall were closed doors. Moments later, out of one of those doors, an older doctor appeared, dressed in a starched white smock. He had funny-looking hair, and moved with a waddle. As he shuffled into my examining room, he tripped over his work-stool and fell directly across my lap with a thud. Embarrassed, he quickly got to his feet and straightened his outfit.

Grunting a few times, he stammered, "Hmm…let's get some x-rays."

After the films were taken, his nurse took them into the darkroom to process. As we waited, the doctor noticed from my registration form that I went to Brooks Institute of Photography.

"You're a photographer!" he said with glee. "That's my hobby. Let me show you my work."

Returning from his office, he brought a stack of view-sheets for 35mm slides. And what pictures they were! All of his images were of dead and rotting teeth and gums. With great pride, he pointed out his lighting techniques and exposure control. Then he got out his camera case to show me his equipment. All this time, my pain grew deeper, and my mind focused only on fear. Finally, I heard the bell from the darkroom, and knew his x-rays were ready. Thank God!

When he returned with the films, they were still wet, inside a stainless-steel processing holder. As he held them up to his examining light so that we could both see them, the chemicals dripped all over my lap.

"Impacted wisdom tooth… just as I thought," he said looking at the x-rays. Then, turning to me with a manic look on his face, he continued, "Let's take all four of them out, and I'll setup my camera to document the procedure."

That's when his name hit me like a freight train… D. Bumsted! I couldn't get out of that office fast enough! My teeth weren't modeling for his gum shots, and I'd tough out the pain until I could see my family dentist.

After graduation, it was a long drive back to my home town of Portland, Oregon. But D. Bumsted never laid his scalpel in my mouth! †

Chapter 8

Cat Paw

Inspirational Short Story
Inspired by an actual event, this story is fictional

With the clock chiming the first nautical bell, Samuel's pale blue eyes popped open. By the end of the third bell, he had the bedside lamp on and had moved his lanky torso to the edge of the mattress. There, with both feet resting on the worn carpet, he listened to the final three bells. The cold November morning was still dark, and on his roof he heard the rustle of the wind and the dancing of the rain. Rubbing his sleepy eyes, he thought, *A typical stormy day for mariners on the North Coast.*

With that in mind, he stood and looked down at his mahogany, handcrafted, pineapple double bed. His side had been disturbed, while the other side had not. This glance at his empty berth was one of many daily reminders of his beloved wife, Hanna. Turning away with a frown, he shuffled his bare feet into the bathroom.

Switching on the light over the sink, he brushed what remained of his teeth, put in his upper denture, and snarled at his reflection in the mirror. The years had replaced his once-chestnut hair with a thinning ash-gray mop, while his straggly chin whiskers were pure white. Only his bushy, untrimmed eyebrows retained a hint of brown. While his deep-set eyes still had a glint, the lines of his weathered face looked like a roadmap. At seventy-five, he looked and felt old. He shook off this disappointment by removing from the medicine cabinet the three vials of pills his doctor had ordered. These he swallowed, as prescribed, with a glass of water. Why he still cared about taking this medicine, he did not know.

Before dressing, he went into the kitchen and plugged in his percolator. As the little chrome machine started bubbling, he went into the living room, stoked the embers of the fire from the night before, and placed fresh wood inside the black cast-iron stove. As the flames took hold, he moved to his well-worn leather armchair, and switched on the floor lamp next to it. When the light came on, it revealed a room stacked with bundles of old, yellowing newspapers. They filled almost every nook and cranny of the little room. From a stack of papers, he selected a couple from the day before and put them in his leather chair. He then returned to the bedroom.

Ten minutes later, he walked into the kitchen again, dressed in a tattered gray wool turtleneck, stained canvas trousers, and a pair of old ankle-high boots. Pouring himself a mug of coffee, he moved to his chair and sat down. Settling in, he put on his drugstore eyeglass and started reading his old papers. He was a pathetic-looking fellow, with his disheveled gray hair and shabby Goodwill clothes, reading by the harsh light of the floor lamp. His Christian name was Samuel Beck, but he wasn't a church goer. His wife and children had called him Sam or Sammy, but to everyone else he was Mr. Beck or, now, Old Man Beck. The neighborhood kids, who were frightened of him, called him other awful names because of his grouchy disposition and menacing appearance. He didn't like those hateful names, but there wasn't much he could do about it.

As he read his newspapers, there was always a snarl on his face, as if the news was all terrible. Samuel was alone, all alone, and mostly from his own accord. He didn't care much for people, and less for children, even his own. He had two: a daughter, Anna, and a son, Erik. Both grown and gone. The daughter lived in New York City, dreaming of stage lights and a career in acting. As a profession, Samuel couldn't understand it. He had never seen a stage play and considered it a waste of time and money. On the other hand, his son lived in California and was a computer engineer, whatever the hell that meant. Samuel didn't own such a machine and didn't want one. He had always had a head for numbers, and trusted only in his own wits and the slipstick he had learned to use with speed and accuracy. The fact was, his two children were disappointments to him. Both had moved away right out of high school, and neither had a love for the family or the sea. But those bitter feelings were his secret; he had never told such things to his beloved Hanna. How could he? She had reared the children pretty much on her own. He hadn't been much help, as he had spent most of his life at sea.

Samuel rested the newspaper on his lap and removed a smoking pipe from the table-side rack next to his chair. He filled the bowl with some Carter Hall tobacco and lit it. As white smoke filled the still air, he picked up the papers and started reading again.
In the shadow of the Korean War, Samuel had joined the Merchant Marines in 1950. But before leaving for his first tour of duty, he had married Hanna, in Astoria, Oregon, where they had met on a blind date. They were two peas in a pod, both second-generation Norwegians, both with a love for Scandinavian foods and the great outdoors, and both with a deep respect for each other and the sea. They'd had a honeymoon of just one weekend before Samuel shipped out.
Almost a year passed before he saw Hanna again. In fact, he spent only six weeks ashore in the first three years of their marriage. That was his curse as a seafarer; it was an adventurous, well-paying job, but it was filled with lonely separation. When he did get leave, he and Hanna were like newlyweds again, while their late-in-life children treated him like an unwanted visitor in his own home. This rancor ran deep, and try as he did, he and his kids had never bonded.

Thirty-eight years later, with a chest full of ribbons and a ticket as First Mate, Samuel had retired from the Merchant Marines to claim his dream of spending his remaining years with his wife and family. But that hadn't worked out very well. His kids still resented his many absences and Hanna had taken sick right after his retirement. She suffered from cancer for a number of years, before dying of it a decade ago. With his wife dead and his children gone, Samuel's life had changed forever.

The hall clock struck the half-hour, and he checked the time with his grandfather's pocket watch, at the end of a golden chain. Turning in his chair, he glanced out the window next to him. The rain had let up, and he could see the hint of a new day in the southwest horizon. Standing, he placed his papers back on top of the stack next to his chair and moved to the woodstove. There, he opened the iron doors and tapped his spent tobacco into the firebox. Closing the fire doors, he went back into his bedroom.

Moments later, dressed in a navy-surplus peacoat and an old blue stocking cap, Samuel exited his cottage on Twelfth Street and started walking the ten blocks to his destination. His gait was slow and his shoulders hunched as he moved down the streets. Soon, the sky turned threatening again, and it started to rain with gusto. He paid the foul weather no mind, as he had spent years walking the wet decks of ships and this little gale was but a reminder of the days gone by.

The last time he had seen his children was at Hanna's funeral. Both had protested loudly about the parsimony of her ordinary pine casket, the thriftiness of her headstone, and her interment in an overgrown pioneer cemetery.

"Father, your cheapness has followed mother into her grave," Erik had said, with anger evident on his face.

And Anna had added, "What a damn miser you are, father. You didn't even buy her a decent burial dress."

Samuel had tried to explain to them. "These arrangements were at your mother's request. She wanted to be with her grandparents, and buried as they were. As for her dress, it was her favorite frock, and at her asking. Money played no role in these choices."

But they wouldn't listen, and the rancor swelled up again until it became clear that, in some twisted way, they blamed Samuel for her death. That was the last time they had all been together, and, in his mind, it was the last time they *would* be together.

With rain pelting down on his blue wool coat, Samuel arrived at the donut shop five blocks from his home. He ducked into the store and purchased a day-old donut for fifty cents and a small coffee for another quarter. He ate the fried cake, and drank his brew in the dryness of the shop, watching the squall blow by.

Hanna had started the hoarding of the newspapers. He and his wife were both avid readers. When she'd learned that aboard ship he couldn't get newspapers until they reached a port, she started saving her daily papers for when he returned home. It was a sweet gesture of love and, after her death, he couldn't bring himself to discard her many years of thoughtfulness. Each of the yellowing stacks represented a different year, containing the history of their love, life and times.

As the rain started to let up, he continued on his journey. Just before eight a.m., he arrived on the stoop of the public library. Here he huddled under the front-door roof, waiting for it to open. As he did, he noticed a new poster taped to the backside of the glass entrance. It was another reminder of the city's fundraising efforts to build a new library. But this time there was an artist rendering of what the new library might look like. To him, it looked big and expensive. Samuel had read about this community dream for many years, but he doubted whether the little seaside town had enough rich patrons for such a luxury.

The interior lights came on and, moments later, the librarian unlocked and opened the front door from the inside.

"Come in and get out of the weather," she said, opening it.

Moving through the threshold, with rain dripping from his beard, he replied gruffly, "You need a bigger roof over your front porch."

"You need an umbrella, sir," she replied.

Samuel scoffed. "No damn umbrella allowed on the decks of the big ships."

"Well, the new building will have a large roof," she answered, with a friendly smile.

"You're a dreamer, lady," he retorted. "This back-wash of a port won't ever be able to afford it."

The librarian smiled at him again with a sheepish look.

Samuel had always felt the lady librarian was a little frightened of him because of his appearance. He took up his usual chair in the reference department and started reading the day-old papers. He would remain in his chair until the postman showed up, around noon. With the arrival of more current news, he would take away yesterday's newspapers, with the consent of librarian. He would add these papers to his stacks at home, and read them again the next morning. That was his daily routine, a habit that hadn't changed since the death of his wife.

At noon, as he moved to the checkout counter with his papers in hand, he gazed around the library. It wasn't much of a facility, an old converted house filled with bookshelves, wonky floors, poor lighting and few windows. At best, it was a library. At worst, it was a firetrap.

When he approached the librarian at the desk, he asked sternly, "Can I take these old papers home?"

The middle-aged lady looked at him and nodded her blond head. "Yes," she answered, with a puzzled expression. As he turned to leave, she added, "Sir, I found this in our Lost and Found. It's been here for years. Why don't you take it?"

Samuel turned back to her. She was holding a black umbrella in her hand. Her kind offer caught him off guard, and all he could do was glare back at her.

"It will keep you dry. It's in good shape," she said, and added, "I don't even know your name, sir."

Samuel moved back to the counter and took the umbrella. "Thank you. I'm Mr. Beck. And you would be…?"

"I'm Helen Homes, and I'm pleased to finally know your name. But I have a question. Why do you take the old papers every day?"

"I'll read them tomorrow morning for my wife."

"Is she an invalid?"

"No, she is dead. But I read to her every morning out of love and respect."

For the first time in ten years, they exchanged glances with fondness in their eyes. As Samuel walked home that day, with his new umbrella over his head, he thought again about Helen's generosity.

At home that afternoon, he relit the morning fire, turned on his radio, and prepared his usual lunch. It wasn't much: heating up some wassail on the stove, he opened a can of food that was labeled fish and fowl, and added a few crackers to his plate. Even though he had no cat, he had taken to buying cat food right after his wife's death. It was cheap and tasty.

With a mug of wine in hand and a plate of food, he sat down in his chair to enjoy the Coast Guard chatter about weather and Bar conditions. Just as he was finishing up his meal, he heard a knock on the front door. Setting his plate aside, he slowly moved to the entrance and opened the door with a scowl on his face.

There on his stoop stood a young girl, dressed in a hooded, buttoned-up jacket, holding a white plastic bag. She had pale hair and the biggest brown eyes he had ever seen.

"What the hell do you want?" he demanded.

"Mommy sent me over with some of her chili," she answered meekly. "Can I come in?"

"Why?" Samuel snapped back.

"It's raining out here."

"I'll take it."

"No." The little girl tightened her grip on the bag. "Mommy told me to put it in your kitchen."

"Alright, but don't drip on my carpet."

Pulling back her hood, she moved past him, filling the doorway, and walked into the living room. Samuel turned and followed her. "Kitchen's over here."

"Why do you have all these old newspapers?" she asked walking past the piles.

"That's none of your affair."

In the kitchen, she opened the plastic bag and placed a covered glass bowl next to his stove. "All you have to do is heat it up. Mommy makes really good chili."

He grunted at the little towhead. "Why would she make me food?"

The little girl's big eyes looked around the kitchen. "We're your new neighbors. It's the Christian thing to do."

Samuel snorted at the little girl. "You must be a believer."

"Yes," she answered quickly. "Hasn't Jesus come into your heart?"

"That's none of your business," he gruffly replied.

She noticed all the cat food cans stacked on his counter. "Where's your kitty?"

"I don't have one. I hate pets, but I like eating their food."

The little girl made a sour face. "Ick! Why do you hate cats?"

The little imp was full of questions. Feeling anger build in his chest, Samuel said, "Because they all die."

Her large brown eyes started up at him for a long moment. That was when Samuel noticed something squirming inside her buttoned-up coat. "What's in there?" he asked, pointing at her jacket.

She smiled up at him with a face as bright as a new moon, and unfastened her top two coat buttons. Out popped the head of a calico kitten. The tiny thing looked at him and meowed.

"I found her in the backyard yesterday. She's a feral kitten – that means she was abandoned by her family." The little girl pulled the kitten all the way out from her jacket. "I named her Saltine. She's really a good cat and she won't die for long time."

He snarled at the kitten, but instead of contempt he felt sympathy. The little calico was all alone, just like him.

His visitor handed the cat to him. "Mommy won't let me keep her, so I brought Saltine for you."

Samuel held the kitten and felt his heart melt away like an iceberg in July. "Why would you give me your cat? I don't understand."

The little girl reached out and scratched the kitten's head. Saltine started to purr. "You have all the food she'll need, and a big warm house to live in. All I want is for you to love her and take care of her."

Samuel dropped to one knee, putting himself at the girl's eye level. "What's your name? And why me?"

She appeared to think a moment, looking at him. "They call me Hana. Mommy tells me my names means 'favored by God.' And *giving* makes Him smile."

Those simple words, coupled with her name, sealed Samuel's fate, and his appetite for life strengthened and took hold, like the morning embers in his cast-iron stove.

That night, in bed, he thought about the generosity he had witnessed that day: the umbrella, the chili, the tiny kitten from Hana. As he mulled over those thoughts, a notion struck him like a bolt of lightning. Just as his idea took form, Saltine jumped up on the bed and curled up next to him. Purring, she put her paws on his outstretched arm and, together, they slept the night through.

Getting up the next morning, he glanced down at his handcrafted bed, and saw the kitten still curled up on his wife's side. The frown faded from his face, replaced by a smile as he started his new day.

Later, when he had trimmed his beard and had done the best job on his hair that he could, he walked into the library with a bounce in his step and a Christmas smile on his face. Seeing that there were no other patrons in the depository, he approached Helen at the check-out counter.

"Good morning," he said. "I would like to make a contribution to the city's library building fund."

Helen looked up from her work with a warm smile. "Good morning, Mr. Beck. I would be pleased to accept whatever you can afford."

Samuel reached into his pocket, brought out a well-worn checkbook, and started writing. As he did, Helen continued, "Next week is Thanksgiving, and I was thinking you might not have anywhere to go. If that's so, I'd like to invite you to have dinner with my family. I'm a good cook when it comes to turkey, and we'd be proud to have you."

He tore the check from his book and looked up at Helen. Her face was filled with sincerity.

Samuel was deeply moved with her kind offer, but embarrassed to tell her the truth. "Thank you for the invitation," he said, "but I'm spending Thanksgiving with my family." Handing her the check, he added, "Please keep this donation anonymous."

She glanced down at the check with a smile…and her face turned to stone. The amount he had written was $500,000.00.

Seeing the shock he had given her, Samuel spent the next hour convincing her that the check was real, and explaining how he had come by such a large sum of money. In the end, he attributed his good fortune to a frugal lifestyle, fifty years of compounding dividends, and his favorite newspaper, the Wall Street Journal.

That evening, with the kitten on his lap, and a roaring fire in the cast-iron stove, Samuel was astonished to receive a phone call from his daughter, Anna, in New York City, asking if she could come home for Thanksgiving. Samuel wholeheartedly agreed. Moments later, Erik called with the same request and with the same results. Hanging up the phone, Samuel contemplated the miracle of giving and receiving, while thinking about a quote by Winston Churchill: "We make a living by what we get. We make a life by what we give." †

Cleft Chins

As a young teen, I followed many 'action hero' type movie stars. Kirk Douglas, Burt Lancaster, Cary Grant, and Robert Mitchum were my favorites. All these men had one thing in common, a deep cleft in their chin. So that's what I wanted! For many months, I went to bed with my chin cleft taped together with Band-Aids. But it didn't work as well as I had hoped, just not deep enough!

My new bride Tess and me - 1972

Chapter 9

When America Worked!

The good old days, right? Well, yes. I recently read a news story about how, today, the start-ups for small business are at an all-time low since the end of WWII. That got me thinking about when my wife and I started our little company.

It wasn't much of a business, just more of an idea at first. I had graduated from Brooks Institute of Photography in Santa Barbara in 1968 and returned home to Portland, Oregon, where I worked as a professional photographer for a number of years. During that time, I secured a small number of faithful clients and developed a reputation as a can-do photographer. My philosophy was simple: Always put your customer first. If they win, you'll win.

With an investment of only fifteen hundred dollars, we opened our doors with two employees in 1972. Media West, Producers of Visual Communications, Inc., was born. Our studio was located in a bad section of town, sharing a building with a small industrial manufacturer. My wife Tess stayed with her full time job, as we knew her paycheck was our life-line. She joined the staff later. We secured a few small assignments right off, and luckily a national client, as well. But it was truly hand-to-mouth, to begin with. Over the next three years, the staff grew to six, with sales over a quarter million dollars.

About this time, my father-in-law, Murray McBride, became our business partner. Murray was a small business guru with deep roots in the Portland corporate community. He was a wonderful guy with a wealth of entrepreneurial information.

At one of our many 'Monday Morning' business meetings, I started complaining again about our cramped studio space, our old photo equipment, and our loud next-door neighbor, the industrial manufacturer.

What Murray suggested that morning was shocking. "Why don't you buy the building and kick the manufacturer out?"

"How?" was my startled reply.

"With an SBA bank loan," he answered nonchalantly.

This guy was crazy. When I walked into banks, they locked the cash drawers! "I would have to remodel the entire building and buy new equipment. No bank in their right mind would make such a loan to me," I said, with my head swimming.

Murray replied confidently, "The Small Business Administration would guarantee such a loan to a local bank, if *YOU* can convince them that our company is worthy of such a loan."

The next day, Murray introduced me to one of his many banker friends. That started it all. Those two men gave me a crash course on the five Cs of banking: **Character, Capacity, Capital, Collateral, and Credit**. After many weeks of hard work and tons of paperwork, our application (a two-inch-thick file folder) was sent to the SBA. A few weeks later, the local bank loaned us enough money to buy, remodel, and equip a new 4,000-square-foot studio, with the SBA (Federal Government) guaranteeing 80% of the loan! But wait… there is NO free lunch: my wife and I had to personally guarantee, to the bank, that the loan would be repaid. Even going bankrupt was not an option. We were on the financial hook for every penny of the load!

Over the next few years, we took out two more SBA loans. All those loans totaled well over one millions dollars. They were all repaid by 1982, and by then we were working directly with the local banks, without the need for SBA guarantees. Media West went on to become one of the largest audio-visual production companies on the West Coast. We had offices in the Bay Area, Seattle, and our brand new 14,000-square-foot headquarters building in Beaverton, Oregon. In our heyday, we had over fifty employees, and revenues in the millions of dollars. But why would the SBA have such a program for our little company? Good question, but think about all the local, state and federal taxes we paid over those years; it was a win-win for the governments, the local banks, and our staff!

Today the SBA program is in shambles. They are plagued with loan defaults and bureaucratic political correctness. Now, to qualify for a loan, you have be some type of a minority or victim, real or perceived. And the new rules and hoops are way too complex, making the program a much bigger challenge. But, *We* did it with just fifteen hundred dollars in start-up capital and faith in ourselves. God bless America! But all this happened back when America worked. The good old days!

Oh, and my philosophy on employee healthcare benefits was also quite simple: we paid half their monthly health insurance premium. After all, it's *their* health care, and all employees need a financial stake in their own wellbeing. †

Honest sweat equity is the best asset any entrepreneur can bring to their business!

The Rabbit That Ran Out of Gas

The first few years in our new business, Media West, were very lean. But, with hard work and luck, I finally landed a few national accounts. One of them was with the Encyclopedia Britannica Company. They were producing a series of 35mm film strips on farmyard animals, the strips were to be distributed to grade-school children. We photographers were given specific assignments about which farm animal we were to photograph. Our assignment was ducks and rabbits.

My job was to read the client's scripts and make sure my photographers had the right props, and breeds of ducks and rabbits. Yes, there are all different breeds of these barnyard animals. Some were easy to find, others quite rare. After searching the countryside for days, I finally had all the breeds secured except one: the English hare. That one seemed impossible to find, until I heard about a breeder down-state who had such a hare. But he was reluctant to rent him to me. After some negotiations, he agreed to release the rabbit to me for twice my rental fee of $75.00.

After a long stormy car trip, I returned to the studio with the English hare secured in his travel hutch. Leaving him with my photographers, who were working through the night to complete the filmstrip, I informed them of his value and how rare a breed he was. They assured me that they would take good care of him.

Returning the next morning, my two photographers rushed into my office with long faces. With sad looks, they ask me to join them.

As we walked back to the studio, Jim, my lead photographer, finally said, "We had a tragedy here, last night."

"What kind of tragedy?" I inquired.

"We were shooting the last frame of the filmstrip, the image of the English hare leaping across the picture. We got him to jump a number of times, but on the final shot, when he came down from his leap, he was dead!"

Henry, the second photographer, added, "I ran into the kitchen and got a straw and tried to give him mouth-to-mouth, but he didn't respond."

The mental image of Henry giving CPR to a rabbit nearly made me laugh.

"Where is he?" was all I could ask with a straight face.

They took me into the kitchen and opened the freezer door. There lay the English hare, as stiff as a board.

"We thought he was valuable because of his pelt, so we froze him," Jim said.

I hadn't had my morning cup of coffee yet, and I didn't know if I should laugh or cry. One thing was certain: the prized English hare was dead, and I was in trouble.

Later, I learned that English hares have weak hearts and can easily become stressed out. Our little guy probably died of a heart attack in mid-air. And yes, we did get the picture. That very last image was used in the final filmstrip.

As for the breeder… we paid him $500.00 and he got the pelt! What was I going to do with it? It would only remind my staff of the rabbit that ran out of gas. †

Chapter 10
Fly Fishing, New Zealand

Author's Note: Over my thirty-five year career as a professional photographer-videographer, I was fortunate to have many dream assignments. This adventure took place in November of 1981 when location video production was just emerging as a reliable replacement for the 16mm film format. The story was featured in a national trade magazine in 1982, with my picture on the front cover. As an avid fisherman, this was a dream assignment for me.

There was definitely something about skimming the tree tops at 120 miles per hour with my new Ikegami 730 video camera and a goodly portion of my not-so-athletic body hanging out of a four-man helicopter, with five passengers and video gear, that made me wish I had both feet firmly planted on my native American soil. At the same time, there was something about this country, these people, and those fish we were after that made me wish it would never end.

New Zealand is, to say the least, a long way from anywhere – 1,200 miles from Australia, 5,000 miles from Asia, and 6,000 miles from the Americas. Its two large islands have a land mass nearly equal to that of Japan, but its population is a sparse three million in comparison to Japan's 118 million. These people are isolated, surrounded by thousands of miles of open sea, and it shows in their self-sufficient, independent attitude; in their culture's blend of Twentieth Century convenience with centuries old tradition; in the pride they take in their beautiful country, and in

their unpretentious welcome to visitors like the four of us.

Besides myself - a videographer with few national, let alone international credits – there was our international tour guide, Mac Beatty, and my two clients, world-class fly-fishing experts and expedition leaders, Randall Kaufmann and Jack Moore. All of us had journeyed more than 10,000 miles, from the chilly winter rains of Portland, Oregon, to the warm spring breezes of New Zealand, to go fishing. We had come to stalk the great brown and rainbow trout that anglers around the world know and covet. (In fact, we learned the Jack Nicklaus had just spent two weeks at one of the fishing camps on our itinerary.) I had come to shoot a video documentary of our experiences for the enjoyment and edification of fishing-club members and anglers who might want Kaufmann and Moore to take them on similar jaunts.

In fact, the video program, I was to make, provided the only evidence that Kaufmann and Moore were world-class, world-traveled fly fisherman – except for a sizable and dog-eared collection of photographs. On their walls, there are no trophies that some taxidermist had artfully posed, and there's not a stringer or creel between them, because they were avowed and very vocal "catch-and-release" enthusiasts.

Kaufmann explains, "To any ardent fisherman, the ultimate experience comes in battling wild game fish, as opposed to those that have been bred and raised in hatcheries. The underlying philosophy of catch-and-release is to conserve the population of wild fish for other sportsmen and future generations to enjoy. Releasing your catch doesn't detract from the sport at all – if anything, it heightens the experience to know you're leaving everything exactly as you found it, without damaging or destroying anything."

The local Kiwi anglers thought us Yankee fisherman were crazy, as they had never heard of the concept of catch-and-release. At the time, New Zealand had no fishing seasons; it was open all year, and there were no bag limits: you took what you wanted. These types of fishing rules were long gone, back in America, and Kaufmann did his best to educate the local anglers.

To call the salmon-sized browns and rainbows "wild" is to understate the case – these fish are legend. Both species were introduced to the waters of New Zealand late in the last century, and they have survived and thrived. It is reported that, in 1904, a Maori (one of the native Polynesian people of the country) speared a brown trout that weighed 51½ pounds. The ones caught during our 14-day trek were smaller – between four and ten pounds, definitely big enough to be "keepers" – but all were returned to the waters from which they had been taken.

Those waters included some of the clearest, quietest, most awe-inspiring lakes, rivers and streams I have ever seen. We reached these fishing grounds by car, on foot, and by helicopter, but I'd had to do some pre-planning before we began our adventure.

First, I researched the power, and discovered New Zealand runs on 220V, 50 cycles. As a result, my American equipment would have to be 100% battery powered. Besides the camera, I took a Sony 4800 video recorder, a fluid-head tripod, shotgun and wireless microphones, a mixer, a color monitor, a battery charger, and a large supply of batteries and blank video tapes. In all, my video equipment weighed over one hundred and fifty pounds. But I soon discovered that the 50-cycle power did not operate the battery charger properly – the batteries could not be fully charged overnight. It is surprising how selective you can become about your shots when you know you have only 90 minutes of power. Next time, I'll take along a transformer or a small generator.

I also consulted with my clients, who were experts on the terrain and weather we were likely to meet, and discovered that we would be going into sections that were rain forests. So I included a couple of items to protect the equipment from moisture – a golfing umbrella and a heavy tarp to use as ground cover. But I forgot the headphones for the audio system – and thus I learned one basic lesson of location production: always make an equipment checklist and check it before you leave and after you arrive, both going and returning.

Another lesson learned: I had cleared all the equipment with United States customs but, when we arrived down under (on a Sunday), New Zealand Customs promptly impounded my equipment. Home-produced commodities are fairly cheap on these islands, but anything imported is extremely expensive. A mid-1970-model used American car, for example, might sell for as much as $20,000. I am sure the customs officers thought I had brought that color TV set so I could sell it and turn a quick profit. They had no understanding of TV standards, and did not realize that the set would not operate on New Zealand power.

Finally, our sponsoring airline, Air New Zealand, had to post a bond of $25,000 before we were allowed to bring our video equipment into the country. By Monday morning, however, everything was cleared, so we could start for the interior (and the airline would get their bond money back when we left two weeks later). Still, the next time I go out of the country for a production, I'll be sure to get in touch with a local import/export broker and fill out the proper forms for International Customs clearance.

When we left in quest of the fish, our journey took us across pastures, into glacier-carved canyons, and over snow-capped mountains. We stayed in small towns or at local fishing camps, and relied on the expert local guides to pinpoint waters which would lend themselves equally well to landing a good catch and getting a good camera angle. The two are not necessarily synonymous. As I soon discovered, fly fishermen do not carry video gear, and fish do not jump on cue. Thus, without an assistant along (a lack I will remedy next time), it was entirely up to me to be unpacked, set up, and rolling by the time their lines hit the water. That is no small task when the helicopter puts you down on a sandbar in the middle of a river.

Likewise, when somebody cried, "Fish on!" I had only seconds to figure out - from my vantage point behind a 2" viewfinder - where it was, which way it was likely to run, and when it might break water for that classic shot which every fisherman cherishes. My in-focus average on the "jump" shots was about one in four. Shooting an NBA playoff game would have been easier, but not nearly as exciting as watching the fierce, yet friendly, duel between fish and fisherman.

The fish usually lost, but rarely have the captured been treated so kindly. These men really cared, which became obvious as I watched them gently cradle each catch just under the surface of the water while it rested and regained its strength. According to Kaufmann, "The whole ritual of selecting the proper fly,

stalking the fish, feeling it strike, then playing it and landing it is extremely exciting. But to me, it is even more exhilarating to release the fish from the line, carefully revive it, and then let it go."

The "ritual of selecting the proper fly" can be deceptively simple, especially to those who, like me, have trouble deciding between a worm and a salmon egg. What Kaufmann and Moore do is kneel at the edge of the water and turn over rocks to see what kinds of insects are indigenous to that particular stream. Then they merely pick one of their hand-tied creations that matches what they find. It seems hardly fair to the fish, but it works.

What they call "stalking the fish," I call "double-teaming." In places where the angler does not have a clear view, his teammate finds a better vantage point and tells him exactly where to cast. Again, hardly fair to the fish, especially in New Zealand's crystalline waters where you can spot the quarry in pools that are up to 15 or 20 feet deep. There is just no place to hide.

During our two weeks, I shot and they fished dozens of locations, from Lake Taupo and its many tributaries on the North Island to the Karamea River and the mountain streams on the South Island. The weather was beautiful the entire time, and when a sudden spring rainstorm hit on the afternoon of our last day out, it didn't really bother anyone.

By that time, I had six hours of tape safely packed away in my case. Not all of it was about fish; some of it showed the local people as they gathered at all kinds of accommodations, from luxury resorts to family run boarding houses, to talk about fish, beer (a point of local pride), and the New Zealand way of life. Other footage was of the magnificent scenery, aerial shots from the helicopter, sunsets over the Tasman Sea off South Island, the Rangitaiki River on North Island, or the icy streams from the Southern Alps that feed Lake Tekapo that brim with trout. My next task was to edit all of this down to a mere 26 minutes, and the choices were going to be tough.

After returning to the States, the post production of that 26-minute video took well over two weeks of working in a darkroom with sound and video editing equipment. The final program, 'Fly Fishing New Zealand,' was mostly about the country and its people, intercut with the record of our fishing trip.

For the audio track, I purchased a record of native Maori music before we returned, and used it under the opening titles and as background for some of the scenic sections. The narration was professional, but the voices of Kaufmann and Moore talking about the fishing were from the location tapes. I had used the shotgun mic to pick up ambient sounds, like the splash of the fish as they jumped, and those were also edited in as natural background audio. (Incidentally, the recording of the splashes did not work too well. We re-created those during post production by sloshing a

hand in water, which gave a more satisfactory sound.)

We sold 'Fly Fishing New Zealand' into the 'home video' markets for a number of years. Had the program been produced thirty years later, we would still be seeing it on 'reality' cable television shows. This was a dream assignment for me, but I soon returned to my love of salmon fishing, because I like to eat my catch! †

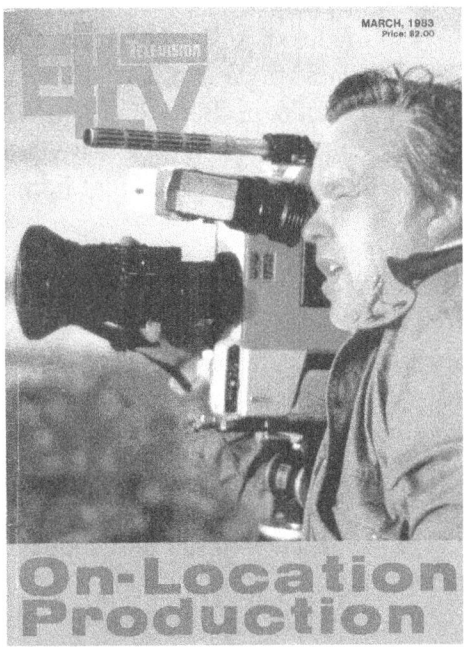

Postscript: Not long after returning to America, we learned that the helicopter we flew with during our adventure had crashed killing our pilot. The reason for the accident was listed as the helicopter being 'overloaded.' This was a sad footnote to our journey down-under.

Martial Law

As many of my friends can attest, I'm a jokester. I've always had a good sense of humor and love a good laugh. But, sometimes this fun can come at the expense of a friend or good natured victims. The only rule for my pranks is nothing hateful, dangerous or frightening.

Our company, Media West, produced visual communications that included multi-media slide shows which were big business before the advent of videotape. One of our vendors was a company in Minneapolis, Minnesota, that represented audio-visual equipment made in Europe. Each year, they would send a sales rep to Portland to showcase the latest and greatest inventions from overseas. Their company rep was a large man, a Korean War Veteran, that I enjoyed very much.

During one of his spring time visits, I picked him up at the airport and drove him downtown to his hotel. While we were crossing one of the many tall bridges of Portland, I noticed that the Navy fleet had arrived to help celebrate the Rose Festival Parade. This annual event had been going on for almost a hundred years. On this particular day, there were over a dozen warships tied up at the downtown seawall. In the early morning light, it was a glittering example of the might of the U.S Navy.

"Why are all the Navy ships in town?" my salesman friend asked.

"Food riots," I answered with a straight face.

He glared back at me in disbelief. "I didn't hear anything about this in Minneapolis, this morning."

"You wouldn't," I answered smiling. "The city is under Martial Law, and all news is blacked out."

"Wow!" he said with a worried look. "Will the hotel have food? Will I be safe?"

By the time we arrived at his hotel, I had told him the truth. Later that evening, we had some wonderful laughs about my tale of the Rose Festival Fleet. He and I remained dear friends for many years. †

Chapter 11
Hair-Raising Heights

Portland, Oregon, and Vancouver, Washington, are separated by the mighty Columbia River, so these two cities are connected by a long drawbridge known as the Interstate Bridge. During the nineteen forties, both these communities had huge shipyards that built an assortment of ships for the war effort.

By the late sixties, however, most of these shipyards had been abandoned or torn down. What remained were only rusty ways and the skeleton buildings of the past. But in Vancouver there was still one working yard. It was building gigantic floating platforms for off-shore oil drilling in the Alaskan waters. These platforms were built of steel pillars which were hundreds of feet long and high; they could be flooded with sea water, to sink the rig upright, once it was positioned over the oil drilling site. These massive tubes of water-tight steel were constructed on the shipyard ways, launched into the Columbia River, and then towed by tugboats to Alaska. This was a big operation that employed hundreds of steel workers.

In 1968, after graduating from photography school, I was fortunate to secure a job with Photo-Arts Studio, the largest commercial studio in Portland, Oregon. But I was the low man on the totem pole, the seventh photographer of seven, and so I got all the crummy assignments that the others didn't want.

The hair-raising adventure that followed is as vivid to me today as it was almost forty years ago. It was a typical March day, dark and gray, with rain in the air. When I got to the studio that morning, I learned that an oil platform, being towed down the Columbia River, had collided with the Interstate Bridge while passing under its massive vertical lift. There was a lot of water in the river at that time of year, and the construction company had miscalculated the height for the huge platform to pass safely under the open bridge. I was quickly dispatched to photograph the damage to the bridge from ground level. I tried but, because of snarled traffic from the accident, I had to return to the studio. After a few phone calls, I was sent to catch a helicopter to take aerial shots of the damage. The chopper waiting for me was a small two-seater, without doors, with a young pilot flying it.

We were soon hovering alongside the still-jammed-up lift spans, with me half-resting on the chopper seat and half-standing outside on the landing struts. Using a long lens and my Hasselblad camera, I shot a few rolls of black and white film of the extensive damage to the bridge. From where I was perched, I could look down and see thousands of cars in both directions, stalled in one massive traffic jam. Then I became aware of the bridge crews scurrying around the steel frames, trying to get the span to close across the fast-flowing Columbia River.

Ever since I was a kid, I've had a form of acrophobia, but my condition isn't a fear of heights, it's an irrational desire to jump! On this day, I had to fight off these urges with all of my strength. It all seemed so unreal, the whirling of the blades, the pitching of the helicopter, and the abstract views far below. Thankfully, I finally took my last shots, and we turned for home.

As we approached the Portland skyline, the helicopter radio came alive, and we were told to fly to Vancouver and pick up the foreman of the construction company. Then we were to chase down the tugboats towing the floating platform, and get pictures of any damage to the oil rig. As we veered off for Vancouver, I asked the pilot about the feasibility of three people in a two-person chopper.

"No problem," he answered through the headset. "I've done it before. My concern is gas and losing the daylight. This bird isn't cleared for night flying."

That's just great, I thought. No light and no gas, and the three of us marooned on some deserted sandbar on the Columbia River!

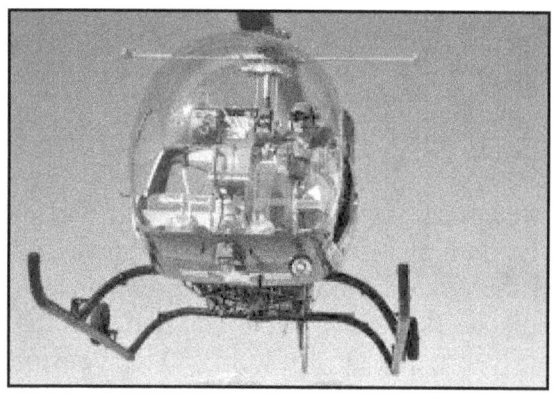

The foreman we picked up was a giant of a man. He had to weigh over two-hundred and fifty pounds. Putting him in the center of the chopper bench seat, the pilot and I flew with half our butts hanging outside the open doors. It was a long, cold, miserable ride down river, with the little helicopter motor humming overtime.

By the time we caught up with the tugboats, they were just starting to cross the Columbia River Bar, which is one of the most treacherous nautical crossings in the world. With the chopper overweight, we found a large sandbar and dropped off the foreman. After I took my pictures, the helicopter would return and drop me off, so the foreman could go up and get a look himself.

When we finally caught up with the floating platform, they were just crossing the Bar in the fading light. The Bar conditions were swirling winds, choppy seas, and light rain. The top of the rig, which had hit the underside of the bridge, was a good two-hundred feet above the churning waves. As we approached the target, I stood outside on the landing struts, with my butt in the open door so the pilot's right hand could hold onto the back of my belt to keep me from falling out. With the winds roaring, the surf pounding, and the chopper twisting in every direction, we made three passes across the top of the big rig. Holding onto my camera for dear life, I snapped off my pictures and fought off those damn urges. It was a bird's-eye view like no other, and I prayed that my exposure was correct. The damage to the rig seemed minimal to me, but what the hell did I know? I was just the photographer!

In a small rain squall, I was dropped off on the sandbar. As the helicopter flew away with the foreman, I stood alone on the windswept beach with a rising tide. The island was getting smaller with every tick of the tide clock. With the light fading and the waters rising, I was finally picked up, half an hour later. In another few minutes, I would have had to swim for shore.

We had just enough fuel and light to make it back to Portland. Looking back at this assignment today, I realize that I was too young and dumb to count the many times we cheated death that day. As for my pictures, they turned out fine, with a few of my prints making into the local newspapers. But dry, firm land never looked as good as it did at the end of that hair-raising heights assignment. †

The Fat Brown Envelope

Over the years, our company, Media West, has had many wonderful clients, a number of which were advertising agencies. One of these firms approached me in the late seventies about producing television commercials for a large retail client with statewide outlets. For these TV spots, the retailer wanted to use a very famous, nationally recognized football star as their spokesman. After a few meetings, and with final budget approval, this commercial production was awarded to our company.

The afternoon before the shooting was to begin, my secretary (today called an administrative assistant) informed me that I was to join my agency contact and his client for drinks at a renowned local bar. *How nice*, I thought on my way downtown. *Just the way all good jobs should start!*

Arriving at the bar, I found my clients having a delightful time. But I was neither asked to sit nor invited to have a cocktail. Instead, I was instructed to drive out to the airport to pick up the famous football star.

"Bring him back here for a drink," the retailer said, reaching into his suit pocket. "And you'll need this." Pulling out a fat brown envelope, he tossed it my way.

"What's this?" I inquired.

"It's his fee. Twenty thousand in cash." (That would be about fifty thousand, in today's money.) "He requires it when he steps off the plane," my agency friend responded.

Bewildered, I nodded and departed for the airport. Driving down the freeway, I was nervous as hell, with all that money on me. What if I had an accident? What if I was mugged? What if the guy didn't show up?

An hour later, I waited for the star at his arrival gate. When he got off the jetway, he was swarmed with fans looking for autographs. Pushing through the crowd, with an outstretched hand, I introduced myself.

He turned my way and simply asked, "Do you have something for me?" When I handed him the fat brown envelope, he grinned, and we both hustled out of the airport.

He turned out to be a nice guy and easy to work with. Our TV spots turned out fine and everyone seemed pleased. But I've always wondered whether our football star slept with that fat brown envelope under his hotel pillow. †

Chapter 12
The Fourth Reich
Short Story

Berlin, Germany - 14 November 1944

A whistle shrieked as the train approached the Central Station. Moments later, in a cloud of white steam, it rolled to a loud, rumbling stop. The first off the front carriage was an SS Colonel wearing a gray wool overcoat, and dressed in his black and silver uniform with twin lightning bolts on his collar and a skull emblem on his cap. He carried but a single suitcase as he stepped down onto the station platform. Turning and walking toward the crowded terminal he noticed snow flurries drifting down from above. Glancing skyward, he saw the problem; the once beautiful, massive glass dome was in shambles from the Allied bombings. *What a shame*, he thought. *Lehrte Station was one of the jewels of Germany.* Pushing his way through a mostly uniformed crowd, he approached the station entrance and found an SS Sergeant holding a placard with his name on it.

Approaching the man, he said in a firm voice, "I'm Colonel Kobl."

The Sergeant instantly snapped to attention, clicking his heels together, while giving the Nazi salute. "Yes, sir. I'm Oberschar-führer Schmidt, your driver. Let me have your bag, sir, and I'll take you to the General."

The two men pushed their way through the hordes of people in the station, and walked outside to a parked black Mercedes. In the dim afternoon light, the Sergeant held the rear door open, and the Colonel slipped into the back seat. As he did, Schmidt noticed his youthful face, cold blue eyes and a jagged ruby scar that ran from above his collar to just under his left ear. The Oberst[1] Kobl had tasted war first-hand, and Schmidt knew

---

[1] Colonel

immediately that this was not a man to be trifled with, but he was so young to have become such a high-ranking officer.

In fact, at just twenty-eight years old, Rolf Kobl was the youngest Colonel in the entire SS. With the help of his influential family, he had risen through the ranks quickly. But now, with most of his relatives dead and their power tarnished from political infighting, he worried about his future. Why had he been called back from the Eastern Front?

With a light dusting of snow on the roads, Schmidt maneuvered the sedan towards the downtown district.

From the backseat, the *Oberst* asked, "Are we going to headquarters?"

Without looking back, Schmidt answered, "No, sir. The General is working from Lion's Lair, these days. It's much safer. There is a thermos of hot coffee in the seat pocket, sir. It will take us about an hour to get to his estate."

With the hot brew in hand, the Colonel stared out the car window and watched the neighborhoods go by. With a light blanket of snow, Berlin looked almost pristine, the sidewalks filled with bundled-up Berliners moving along the avenue. Then his eyes glanced up to the jagged dark skyline, and he was appalled to see the outline of so many crumbling buildings. While the main thoroughfares were passable, many of the side streets were closed, littered with rubble from all the bombings.

Two years had passed since he was last in Berlin, and much had changed. When he had arrived on the Eastern Front in July of 1942, he had found only victories. Country after country, town after town, had fallen under control of the Nazis. His orders had been to oversee the final solution to the 'Jewish question,' so his SS units had built hundreds of concentration and labor camps, and filled them with enemies of the state. Today, all he found on the Eastern Front was defeat, and his SS units were engaged in scorching the earth, leaving nothing for the advancing Russian armies to find. As he glared at the skyline, even Berlin now looked defeated. He sat back in his seat with a scowl on his chiseled face. *How can this be? The Third Reich was to last for a thousand years.*

It was dark by the time the Mercedes pulled up to huge iron gates guarded by two enlisted SS soldiers. His orders and identification were checked with a flashlight by the sentries before the sedan was allowed to enter the compound.

Once the car had pulled up in front of the large, darkened manor, the Colonel got out and walked up the long, snowy flight of stone steps toward the front door. Looking skyward, he could just make out the silhouette of Lion's Lair, the General's estate.

A grin stretched his lips. He had been here many times before, as a child, and he had only fond memories of his uncle, the General, and his home. So why had he been recalled?

The Sergeant was at his heels, and the front door was opened before they could knock. Standing just inside the darkened foyer was a matronly looking woman, holding an oil lamp.

"Come in quickly," she said in a firm voice.

As soon as the men crossed the threshold, the door was closed and the interior lights turned back on.

Putting her lamp on a table, the woman gestured toward a set of closed doors. "Colonel, the General is waiting for you in his study."

Removing his overcoat and straightening his uniform, Kobl knocked firmly, slid open the large oak doors, and entered the room. Once inside, he paused and closed the doors behind him before turning again to face the room. Coming to attention, he clicked his jack boots together and gave the Nazi salute, saying loudly, "Colonel Rolf Kobl reporting as ordered, sir."

The Commanding General of the SS, the Protector of the Third Reich, Reichsführer[2] Karl Hanke stood up from behind his enormous desk and returned the salute. "Heil Hitler," he said, just as loudly.

The General was in his early sixties, dressed in an open grey tunic and tan jodhpurs. A monocle covered his left eye. He moved to the front of his desk and then towards the Colonel with his hand extended.

"Good to see you again, Nephew," he said, shaking Kobl's hand. "But you're late. I expected you this morning."

His grip was firm and friendly. "We Germans don't seem to keep our trains on schedule anymore, sir," Rolf replied with a smile. "Anyone would think there was a war on."

The General pulled his nephew close and gave him a hug.

As they embraced, the Colonel looked around the large, familiar room. On the left were three tall windows that faced the front of the manor, covered with black-out curtains. Across the room was a large crackling stone fireplace, with the family crest hanging above the mantle. On the right was the General's massive oak desk, covered with papers and files. Behind the desk, on the wall, hung a twenty-foot Nazi flag. The other sparse furnishings in the room rested on polished wood floors covered with plush rugs.

As they parted, the General stared soberly at his nephew for a long moment. "I tried to help my brother, your father, but he had gotten in too deep. The Fuehrer was determined to make him an example. After his execution, your mother collapsed and died from a massive stroke. There was nothing I could do, lad."

Kobl stared at his uncle's wrinkled, weathered face and finally, sadly, replied, "You and my sister are the only family that I have now, sir."

"You also have the Comrades," the General replied. "The SS is also your family."

"Yes, sir," Rolf said grimly. "But you are safe here at Lion's Lair, and she is safe in Stockholm with her diplomat husband. So, Uncle, why am *I* here?"

---

[2] Highest rank of the SS

The *Reichsführer* gestured to a single chair in front of his desk. "Have a seat, Colonel. We have much to cover, and only a few short hours."

As the men came to rest in their chairs, the General reached into a desk drawer and brought out a bottle of Cognac and two glass snifters. As he poured the nectar, he asked, "So, Rolf, how is your Spanish?"

"A little rusty, sir," Kobl answered, startled.

The General smiled broadly as he handed the Colonel his drink. "Well, you will soon be fluent." Then his expression darkened. "Tell me, Rolf, how have things been going on the Eastern Front?"

There was no honest way to soften the truth. "Horribly, sir. The Fuehrer's 'scorched earth' policy has my men distracted from their work at the camps, and thousands of the Jews linger on. The skies are full of Russian planes. Where are the wonder weapons promised by Goring?" With some hesitation, the General replied, "There is a new jet aircraft being flown by Luftwaffe, but it is a dangerous machine to fly and we have only a few veteran pilots that can fly them. Our new rockets, the V-1 and V-2's, are now raining down on England, but they have no guidance system, and so they often only fall upon farmer's fields. A new fleet of advanced U-boats is being built, but that is happening slowly. Only a handful are now on duty in Norway. We had planned a battle for the Western Front, using the latest King Tiger Tanks, but the supporting troops were too few and too inexperienced, and they have no proven leadership.

In 1942, we should have finished England off first, made peace with America, and then invaded Russia," the General finally stated, with a long face.

"What are you really telling me, sir?" his nephew demanded.

"Have another drink, Rolf." The General handed the Cognac bottle across the desk to the Kobl, then shook his head. "The war is lost. And, from the ashes of the Third Reich, *we* will build the Fourth Reich."

Pouring the brandy slowly, the Colonel could not believe his ears. His eyes darted around the room as he wondered whether they were being filmed or recorded. But no, the General's treasonous words must be true; no one would dare entrap *Reichsführer* Karl Hanke. He was the third most powerful man in Germany.

The General went on to explain, with a sadistic smirk, how the SS had looted hundreds of millions of Reichsmarks from the Jews. "First we confiscated their businesses, and seized their bank accounts and investments. Then their homes and all their belongings were sold off. But we kept their jewelry, art, and all their valuables. Hell, the SS has an art collection bigger than Goring's. Then we sent them off to the camps where we took their clothes and whatever else they tried to smuggle in. Next, we worked them to near death for the Fatherland. Even in the pigs final butchery, we took the gold from their teeth and their hair for rope. Half of all this booty we shared with the government. The other half, the SS kept. That money is now secreted in numbered banks accounts in dozens of other countries. Our only regret is that we ran out of time before we could complete the Jewish solution. But time is a luxury we no longer have. Now, we must save our own."

The General leafed through a stack of papers on his desk and pulled out a thick manila folder. "With the war lost, we have formed a secret brotherhood called the Odessa[3]. It will provide money, new identities, transportation and safe-houses all around the world for thousands of SS officers and men who need to escape the grasp of the Allies. These soldiers will become the vanguard of the Fourth Reich. You and many others like you will be the keepers of National Socialism, the future of our Fatherland." The General handed Kolb the folder. "I will not order you to take this new assignment, as I realize it is a direct violation of your oath to the Fuehrer. However, if you agree, here are your new orders. Read them and commit them to memory."

Rolf opened the folder and found written orders, along with new identity cards, passport, birth certificate, airplane tickets and a wallet with a few thousand Argentine banknotes. All of those documents bore the name of Axel Garcia, but the picture on the passport was one of himself, dressed in civilian clothes.

"Why Argentina, sir?" the Colonel asked.

"The Argentinean government will welcome Odessa warmly, as they want to take back the Falkland Islands from the British, after the war. We just might help them with a few of our newest U-boats."

"Have the Fuehrer and Himmler signed off on this, sir?" Rolf asked.

"Nein. They are zealots who believe the war is still winnable," the General said. "But Deputy Führer Martin Bormann and a few other high ranking officers have done so. Will you join us?"

Rolf swirled his Cognac glass, lost deep in thought. He hated Hitler for what he had done to his family… but he loved his country. "Aye, sir" he finally said firmly. "The Odessa is my family now. Send me as many Aryan brothers as you can. "

The Colonel was given a suitcase filled with business clothes that fit him perfectly. He was told to establish safe houses not only in Argentina, but in Paraguay, Bolivia and Peru as well. That was to be accomplished by using a front business, called the South American Mining Company, and four million dollars, stolen from the Jews, which he would find waiting in a numbered account in the Bank of Buenos Aires. "The bank codes are in your orders. Memorize them, and then destroy them. Set your networks up carefully, Colonel. Always stay close to the local German communities, as they can be trusted."

Within a few hours, Rolf Kolb, dressed as businessman Señor Axel Garcia, was back in the Mercedes, rushing to the Berlin station to catch the express train to Zurich.

---

[3] Organization of Former SS Members

Buenos Aires, Argentina - 20 November 1944

Señor Axel Manuel sat nervously in his airline seat as the DC3 made its final approach to the Buenos Aires airport. As he looked out the window at the sun-drenched city below, he realized he had traveled from the brutal winter weather of Europe to the middle of the South American summer in just four days; the wonderment of air travel! But, it had been an arduous journey. To begin, he had traveled from Berlin to Zurich via train and then flown Swiss Air to Lisbon. From there, he had boarded the Pan American Clipper to Brazil, where he changed planes to an Aero Argentina flight for Buenos Aires. Everything had gone as planned; his forged papers had been checked numerous times, with no problems. Even his rusty Spanish had improved, once he boarded the Clipper in Portugal. His confidence was building, but he was still nervous and tired. The last hurdle was yet to come: Customs and Immigration at Ezeiza Airport.

When the plane came to rest at the International Terminal, the passengers disembarked down outside stairs and were herded inside along a dingy corridor to the Customs area. As Axel walked along, carrying only his single suitcase, he felt a bead of cold sweat run down his forehead from his Panama hat band. Stopping to take out his handkerchief, he blotted the moisture dry, reminding himself not to talk too much and not to look anxious. Resuming his march, he kept a nonchalant expression on his young face.

The government room was big and bright, with a long row of tall desks in front of Customs Agents, with armed guards watching the arriving passengers. Axel got in line and patiently waited for the next official. When his turn came, he approached a skinny fellow in a wrinkled and stained uniform, with a long, bony nose and wire-rimmed glasses. Handing the man his passport, Axel chuckled under his breath; all bureaucrats looked the same, no matter the country.

The official didn't look up from his passport, and checked the back pages for customs stamps.

"Anything to declare?" he asked, with his nose still down.

Axel answered indifferently, "Nada."

The official held up the photo page of his passport and looked at him carefully. Then, lowering the document, he quickly endorsed one of the back pages with both a customs and an immigration stamp. "Welcome home," he said, handing the passport back.

Axel took the papers and placed them in his valise, then turned and started to walk away. He had only taken a few steps before the agent said loudly, "Señor, I have a question."

Twisting back to the official, Axel answered, "Yes?"

The agent pointed to the side of his own neck, "How did you get your scar?"

Without hesitation, Axel answered, "Esgrima[4]."

---

[4] Fencing

The agent nodded his head with a grin. "Have a good day sir."

Axel pushed his way through the hordes of the main terminal and soon found himself outside in the bright late-morning sun. He stopped curbside and reflected on what had just happened. It was as if a load of bricks had been lifted from his shoulders. He had completed the first part of his mission: he was safely inside Argentina. But now what? He thought of hailing a cab for downtown, and finding a hotel room where he could sleep.

A whispering German voice came from behind him. "Good morning, Colonel. I have a car waiting. But we speak only Spanish in it."

Axel quickly did an about-face and found himself facing a lady in a red, floppy, felt hat. With her auburn hair, high cheekbones and deep-set green eyes, she was a strikingly beautiful woman. Her complexion looked suntanned or Latin, with bright red full lips, little makeup and a shapely figure covered by a conservative feminine business suit. Axel was momentarily speechless.

Finally he mumbled, "Who are you?"

The lady flashed a grin and whispered back, "General Hanke asked me to take you under my wing. I will explain everything at your hotel. Let's get in the car. And remember – speak only Spanish."

Her German was faultless and she sounded native-born. Axel decided to trust her, but only because she had used the Reichsführer's name.

Their taxi sped down a few highways for La Plata, a small community a few miles south of Buenos Aires. From the backseat, their Spanish conversation was limited and only staged for the ears of the driver. When they got to the small town, Axel noticed that many of the street and business names were in German. The lady told him that the area had a large colony of German Nationals who had immigrated to Argentina after the humiliating defeat of WWI. The Colonel liked the news, as it made him feel a little more at home.

The hotel was a four-story white stucco affair, with red roof tiles and black wrought-iron verandas. The street that fronted the hostel was shade-tree lined, with cobblestoned sidewalks that were as clean as a starched bed sheet. Coming from war-torn Europe, Axel was impressed by the picturesque setting of La Plata.

After the driver was paid, the couple walked into the hotel together. The lady had already registered him and had paid for a one-week stay, with another week as an option. All that was required of him was to sign the registration form.

At the front desk, she whispered in his ear in a provocative way, "Your new name."

The desk clerk gave them a strange look, and for the first time the Colonel signed his new name, Señor Axel Garcia. He was handed a key for a room on the third floor, and the couple moved towards the stairs.

"You go on up," the lady said. "I have to make a few phone calls."

Axel found his room large, dark and stale, but clean. All the curtains had been pulled, to keep the heat out. These he swiftly opened and then walked around, opening several windows and the door to the veranda. The apartment quickly brightened, and the musty smells soon dissipated. A few moments later, as he was finishing up in the bathroom, there was a knock at his door.

Opening it he found the lady in the hall, with her index finger to her lips. She shook her head and mouthed, "No talking." Pushing past Axel, she entered the room and started looking under lamp shades and behind pictures. She even unscrewed the mouth piece for the phone. Then she went out onto the balcony and looked around at the neighborhood, two stories below.

Returning, she said in German, "We can talk freely."

Axel took a chair next to a built-in desk, and looked up at the lady. "Who the hell are you, Fraulein?" he demanded.

The lady walked to the room door and locked it, then came to rest on a white, overstuffed chair. Taking off her hat, she crossed her long, shapely legs and asked, with a disappointed look, "You don't remember me, Colonel?"

"Nein," he sternly answered. "And no more games."

The Fraulein took an ivory cigarette holder from her purse and placed an American Camel cigarette in it. She lit her smoke with a silver lighter and then tossed it to Axel.

"Look at the inscription, Colonel."

Axel looked at the lighter. One side was engraved with a swastika; the other side, twin lightning bolts. He had one just like it! It was a handcrafted Swiss Zippo, given to all new SS officers when they were inducted into the Brotherhood. "How can this be?" he asked, confused.

"We have met before, Colonel. You, Himmler, and your father attended my swearing-in ceremony in 1941. I remember it well. To have Himmler, your father who had the ear of the Führer – and you, a handsome young SS Lieutenant, in the audience had my class on Cloud Nine!"

The Colonel worked his memory and then, with a bright face, chuckled. "Yes, I remember now. Heinrich told me that it was the first time a few women were allowed to join the Brotherhood."

"And I was one of them," the lady said proudly.

"The Reichsführer also told me that all the women had outlandish nicknames."

"Mine was Scorpion, and it is still my code name."

"The spider that kills its own."

"I prefer the eighth sign of the Zodiac. It doesn't sound so deadly," she replied with defiant eyes.

"Either way, it is not much of a compliment for such a pretty Fraulein. What is your given name?"

"Nicole López is my Latin name; Nicole Lang is my German name. My father was a low-level Argentine diplomat in Berlin after the First War. He married my German mother in 1920. I arrived shortly after that."

"Where is he now?"

Her expression soured, and she looked away with a frown. "It doesn't matter. He was a man of little intelligence and less importance. After his posting expired, we moved to Argentina. Sometime later, he was killed by a political rival, after which, Mother took me back to Germany, where I was raised."

"How did you end up back here?"

"Simple enough," she answered, with authority written on her face. "The SS posted me here in '43. I'm the Government Relations Envoy for the German Embassy."

"Why all the cloak and dagger behavior?"

"The current government has a secret police that rivals our Gestapo. They like to know what's going on, so being cautious is a way of life here."

There came a knock on the door, and muffled Spanish words, which startled the Colonel. Nicole smiled at him and got up from her chair. "I have taken the liberty of ordering you some lunch," she said, walking to the door. "I know you must be tired and hungry."

The bellboy pushed a white-table clothed cart into the room and set it up next to the open veranda door. Nicole paid him and he was swiftly out of the room, after which she locked the door again.

The Colonel got up and moved to the cart. Looking down at it, he saw an ice bucket with three brown bottles of beer, some condiments and a single plate covered with a cloche. Removing it, he found a thick roast-beef sandwich on rye, with sauerkraut and pickles.

As Nicole walked over to the table, he asked, "Are you not joining me?"

She shook her head. "Nein. I have another engagement. You eat while I tell you about my role in your mission."

The Colonel wasn't sure he liked her superior tone, but he was famished. Moving quickly to his chair, he sat down and opened a bottle of beer.

"You will find the Argentine beef outstanding, the bread marginal, and the sour cabbage good. But it is our beer that you will enjoy the most," she said, and then launched into a long, detailed account, pacing the floor as she talked, and smoking one cigarette after another. She had a direct, secure communications with Germany, she assured him. All messages the Colonel received or sent would go through her. Axel's code name, she said, would be Condor, just as hers was Scorpion, and his outgoing messages would be limited to ten words, mostly code words. She knew the general details of his mission, and she would act as the security officer for the Argentine Odessa. "You will tell me everything you know, and when you learned it," she demanded.

"Why is there a need for a security officer?" the Colonel asked, spreading mustard on his sandwich.

Scorpion smiled broadly and raised her left arm, pushing back the short sleeve of her blouse. "Do you still have your blood type tattooed under your arm? I do not."

"Yes, it is an SS custom."

"Those identifying marks, and any others, such as the scar on your neck, will have to be removed. There is a local doctor who we can trust to erase them, but that will take some time. And Odessa wants no trouble from the current Farrell government. They are not our allies, as yet. But next year there will be an election, and the current Vice President, Juan Perón, will be elected the new President. Then we will have an ally we can trust. Until then, Colonel, you will need a security officer." She continued with a long list of general warnings, then changed the subject to the next few weeks. Her first objective was to secure a small local villa where he and other brothers could be trained and live safely. Then they would find a small office for their front company, the South American Mining Company. "Along the way," she said, stopping to stare at the Colonel, "I will also clean up your atrocious Spanish. Your words are filled with a German accent. For that reason, when I leave here today, you will not go downstairs or walk around the neighborhood. Use room service, and we will begin with lessons in the morning. Do you understand me?"

The Colonel, just finishing his sandwich, glared up at her. Opening the second bottle of beer, he asked, "And what SS rank do you hold?"

"Captain," she replied proudly.

"You might want to remember that, when you address me in the future. I am not accustomed to taking orders from subordinates."

Annoyance filled her face. "Listen, Colonel, I am your life-line here in Argentina. You will not cross me, nor order me about. Give me your passport. I have something to show you."

The Colonel got up, took his passport from his valise and handed it to her.

She opened the document to the picture page. "See the Argentine crest here, and what is behind it?"

He looked closely to where she was pointing and replied, "Two capital letter S's."

"Yes," she said quickly, "SS's means something special to us, and here in Argentina it means 'Special Selection.' All of our brothers will have passports with double S's. That designation means 'allow-in' to every Immigration official in Argentina. That bribe took me almost a year to arrange, and cost many thousands of Reichsmarks. So you need me, Colonel, a lot more than I need you. My authority is not to be questioned."

With his ire up, he replied, "What happens if Germany is defeated?"

With a sinister grin, she remarked, "I will stay in Argentina, as I have dual citizenship."

She was one insolent bitch, and the Colonel was disappointed with her status. Her return to Germany would have taken care of the problem. But her words were true. "Very well, Captain. You will have my cooperation, but walk softly with your disrespectful tone. Do not trifle with me."

Nicole glared at him for a moment, then reached for her hat. "I have to go. Do you need anything? Cigarettes? More beer?"

"I don't smoke. It's a filthy habit. And I don't usually drink, so nada."

Nicole turned for the door and unlocked it. But as she opened it, the Colonel asked, "Tell me about Argentina and its people."

She closed the door again and looked back at him. "It is a country of poor people and peasants, governed by the rich who live here in Buenos Aires. The ruling class is as corrupt as the government itself. I know where the landmines are, and where the bodies are buried, so you are in good hands, Colonel. I'll tell you more tomorrow, when we get started setting up *our* Odessa network." She opened the door again and walked out, saying in Spanish, "Lock the door behind me."

The Colonel bristled and stared at the closed door for a long moment. Scorpion was an unforeseen wrinkle in his mission. While she was easy to look at, she was hard to tolerate. He didn't like her, and wouldn't trust her. But he did need her. Like the Jews, her time would come. There was no place in *his* Fourth Reich for impertinent women. Women like her were only good for giving birth to more Aryan babies.

Finally, he got up from the table, walked over to the door and locked it. Turning back to the room, he found the ashtray she had been using. Taking it back to the cart, he removed the longest cigarette butt and put it in his mouth. Lighting it, he reached for the last bottle of beer in the ice bucket. He *did* smoke and drink, but only privately. All bad habits were a sign of weakness, and he would not share his with anyone.

Hacienda Canario - 20 December 1944

A few miles south of the city of La Plata, were the rolling hills and rich soil of the Santiago River Delta. There, Señor Axel Garcia sat atop a large gray horse, surveying the forty acres of range and farm land he had recently purchased. Soon the lower half was to be cultivated for growing hops, while the upper half would be fenced for grazing the livestock. The hacienda had been purchased from an anxious woman whose husband was a political prisoner of the current government. She needed money for a bribe to the trial judge and the prosecutor. Once her husband was released, the couple would flee to Brazil. Argentina was a corrupt society but, because of that, Señor Garcia had been able to purchase the estate for a pittance.

He spurred his horse farther down the hill. The last few weeks had been filled with activity. With the help of Nicole López, the Scorpion, he had rented a small office/warehouse in La Plata and staffed it with a trustworthy German woman, Helga

Hahn, as the office secretary. Phone lines had been installed, business cards and letterhead printed and a large sign erected out front that proclaimed 'South American Mining Company.' The ruse of the phony business was almost set.

What was next needed was an Argentine with deep roots in the mining business, so they had hired a sixty-year-old geologist named Bruno Vega. The gray-haired, skinny fellow called himself a geologist. Deep down, however, he was just a wrinkle-faced rock hound. Señor Vega had discovered copper, tin and iron mines all over South America but because of the current economy he hadn't worked for years. He relished the chance of making 'one more great discovery.' With him and his rock samples in the warehouse, the ruse was complete.

Axel had also met with the Vice Present of the Bank of Buenos Aires, to claim his numbered bank account. He was surprised to learn that the money the bank held was in US currency. The *Reichsführer* must have been playing it safe, to have used US funds for the original deposit.

Axel opened a business account and put twenty-five thousand dollars' worth of Argentine pesos into it. He did the same for his personal banking account.

While signing the papers for the accounts, Nicole had said, "You should include my name on those accounts. You never know what might happen."

She was a pushy broad, and Axel was embarrassed that she had said it in front of the banker. "Not now, woman," was his annoyed reply.

She glared back at him with a look that could kill.

In the course of these encounters, Axel's Spanish had improved as well. He now had confidence with his new language and was almost beginning to feel at home. He had received and sent three secret messages to his uncle, the *Reichsführer,* and was making progress with the diplomatic codes. But the news from Germany was not good. The Eastern Front was collapsing, and the Western offensive had yet to begin. Part of him desperately wanted to be in the fight, while another part was happy to be safe in his new homeland. The Fourth Reich now rested firmly on his shoulders.

With the sun low in the sky, Señor Garcia turned his horse for the hacienda. When he neared the compound, he paused for a moment. The setting was quite pleasing: the white stucco house was nestled in a small grove of shade trees, with a driveway that connected to a country road. It was a twenty-mile drive to the office, so Axel had bought himself a used 1938 blue Mercedes, which he kept in a large garage at the rear of the house. There was also a roomy wooden barn, a corral and other outbuildings in the backyard. All these structures needed paint and mending. The former owners had moved out a few years before, leaving the estate in disrepair. The main Spanish-style hacienda was spacious, with four bedrooms, three baths, and a good-sized kitchen connected to a covered veranda. Axel even had his own study, complete with a fireplace and red tile floors. Nicole had thought the property too ostentatious for a mere mining company owner. Her choices had been a few villas closer to town, but they were all so tiny and dingy that Axel had refused. He was not going to live like a peasant, so he bought the estate on the cheap, and renamed it Hacienda Canario. The Scorpion had been furious, but she still hired a middle-aged German couple as his household staff. The woman cooked and cleaned, while the husband tended the livestock and did basic maintenance. They lived out behind the house, in a small cottage of their own. Axel supposed that the office Fraulein and the couple were also spies for Nicole, but he didn't really care.

In the barn, Axel unsaddled the horse and gave it a rubdown. Then he led his mount into a stall and put the feed bag on. As he watched the horse eat, he reflected on his Bavarian youth. He had practically been born in a saddle. There was something majestic about horses, and he was pleased to be riding again, even if it was just an old gray mare.

Axel walked into his hacienda, which was as quiet as a tomb. It was Wednesday, and his staff had the day off. Moving to his study, he poured himself a whiskey and lit an American cigarette from a hidden pack in his desk. Turning on the desk lamp, he sat down and enjoyed the privacy of his vices. He would have to send another message to Germany soon. The codes for the Odessa operation had been approved. Germany called the men fleeing to Argentina 'canaries,' and the radiograms would read something like: *Condor, two canaries by sea, or one canary by air.* When they arrived in-country, they would call an unlisted phone number and simply say, 'Canary,' and give their location so that they could be picked up. Everything seemed to be in place, and he looked forward to having some of his SS brothers around him again.

The desk phone rang. It was the Scorpion, calling from the embassy. "I have news," she said with excitement in her voice. "The Fuehrer has launched his Western offensive. Our forces are on the move, and the Battle of the Ardennes has started. This has been confirmed by the Americans on the radio. They are calling it the Battle of the Bulge. How exciting is that? And I've been summoned to meet with Vice President Perón tomorrow. I'm sure he wishes to personally extend his congratulations to the Fuehrer."

"I wouldn't be too sure," Axel answered. "There has been tension between our two countries lately, so walk softly and call me after your meeting."

"What about our Western offensive? You don't sound excited."

"The *Reichsführer* briefed me on the battle plans before I left Berlin. We'll keep our fingers crossed and our ears open. I'll turn on Voice of America. Call me tomorrow."

Late the next afternoon, Nicole barged through the company's front door and marched straight into Axel's small, drab office, where he was speaking with his geologist.

Axel looked up from his desk with an angry glare. "I told you to phone me."

"What I have to say is not fit for the phone," she said, scowling back.

Axel excused his geologist, and Nicole took a seat, with fire in her eyes. She lit a cigarette and then told the story of her meeting.

"He flirted with me at first, as most men do. Then he told me that a German U-boat Captain, Jürgen Wattenberg had walked into the Argentinian embassy in Mexico City and asked for political asylum. He wanted to know what I knew of this man. Then he hinted that, for a sizable campaign contribution, he might consider the request. His wording was vague, and he had a funny smirk on his face."

"Had you heard of this Captain before?"

"No, so when I returned to the embassy, I did some checking. Captain Wattenberg and twenty other German POW's escaped from an Arizona prison camp, a few days ago. Most of the men have been recaptured. But Wattenberg must have made it to the Mexican border, then crossed and hitch-hiked to Mexico City. What do we do?"

Axel smiled broadly. "Maybe we have our first Odessa Canary. When will you see the Vice President again?"

"Tomorrow at eleven-thirty. He talked about taking me to lunch."

"Good. I'll pick you up at the embassy at eleven, and join you for your meeting. But first, I'll stop off at the bank."

"Won't that seem a little strange?"

"No. Just introduce me as Axel Garcia, a local miner of German descent. I'll do the rest."

The Vice President had a suite of offices in one of the many government buildings in downtown Buenos Aires. The capital edifices were large and impressive, with marble steps and Greek columns. Argentinian flags and large pictures of President Farrell and Vice President Perón were on display everywhere. In many ways, the complex of white buildings reminded Axel of Berlin before the war.

Nicole led them through the maze of offices until they reached the Vice President's suite. She checked in with the main secretary, who had them take a seat to wait. A few moments later, the massive double oak doors to the Vice President's office opened, and Juan Perón and a gorgeous young lady emerged. The Vice President noticed Nicole waiting, and they walked over to her.

"Miss López, how nice to see you again," he said. "I would like to introduce you to my fiancée, Eva Duarte. Eva, Miss López is with the German embassy."

The two ladies shook hands and exchanged an odd glance. They were both beautiful woman, and everyone in the office was staring at them. When Nicole introduced Axel as a local miner of German descent, the two men also shook hands, and Alex found Perón's grip firm and determined.

"Eva, was just leaving. I will walk her to the door and then we can meet," the Vice President said.

Moments later, they were seated in front of the Vice President in his massive ornate office, where soaring windows looked out at the Presidential Palace. Perón was a handsome man, tall, lean and trim as a boxer. His teeth were near perfect and bone white. His face was friendly, with a perpetual smile and probing blue eyes.

Nicole told him what she had learned about Captain Wattenberg, describing how he had walked over one hundred and thirty miles across a desert to make it to the border. "He is a brave man, and the German government hopes you will consider his asylum."

The Vice President turned his gaze to Axel. "So, what is this man to you, Señor Garcia?"

"Nothing really, sir, but I would consider sponsoring him."

"Señor Garcia is prominent in the local German community," Nicole inserted.

"Are you of German decent?" Perón asked.

"Yes, sir. My family immigrated here after the first war. I was born in northern Argentina, where my father worked as a miner. That's how I got into the business."

"So, both of you wish me to grant asylum to this man?" the Vice President asked.

"Yes, sir," Axel said quickly with an earnest face. He reached into his coat pocket and brought out a small brown envelope. "That reminds me, sir. I wanted to make a contribution to your upcoming campaign." He laid the envelope on the desk. "The mining business has been good to me, and I look forward to you becoming our next President."

The Vice President opened the envelope and looked inside. His expression showed that he was surprised by the contents. "Yankee one hundred dollar bills. Are you trying to bribe me?"

"No, sir. I only hope you will *consider* his asylum."

"Why gringo money?"

"The American dollar is fast becoming the international currency, and it is very portable."

The Vice President thought for a long moment, then grinned at Axel. "I approve your sponsorship, Señor, and will grant his asylum." He slid the envelope into one of his desk drawers. "Now, will you join Eva and me for lunch?"

The lunch was delightful. Eva captivated the table for almost two hours. The Vice President was relaxed and friendly, greeting his many admirers at the restaurant. The lunch chatter was light, and the food excellent.

On the drive back to the embassy, Nicole expressed her concerns. "You should trust my instincts, Colonel. I know these people better than you do. Offering a bribe to the Vice President was a foolish idea. He could have had us arrested on the spot."

Alex smiled at her. "I've seen men like him before. Taking your first bribe is hard, but after that they all come easy. Don't worry. Juan Perón has been in government a long time. He knows how to run a banana republic."

On Christmas day, Captain Wattenberg flew into Ezeiza Airport from Mexico City. Both Axel and Nicole were there to greet him. They whisked him away to the hacienda, where Canary Number 1 was taken under the wing of Argentine Odessa. It would take months of tutoring to prepare him to survive in his new environment. Along the way, he would be taught Spanish, the history of Argentina, and the culture of its people. Meanwhile, Axel was pleased to have another warrior under his roof, and they spent hours together, listening to the war news and talking all things German.

It was not the plan of Odessa to buy entry for their men. They would depend on the forged documents provided by the German Odessa. The case of Wattenberg, however, was quite different. He was one of only two U-boat Captains held in American captivity, and his escape made international news. The Americans even proclaimed that he had been recaptured, but obviously this was just Yankee propaganda. The twenty-five hundred dollars paid for his freedom had been worth the price. And Axel had made friends with the next President of Argentina, a relationship he would cultivate.

He didn't have to wait long. After the New Year, he and Nicole were invited to dinner at the private residence of Vice President Perón. Delighted, they promptly accepted. In the expectation that it would be a gala event, they both purchased the proper attire.

On the given evening, at the given time, they nervously stood before the imposing home of the Vice President in a rich neighborhood of Buenos Aires. Axel was dressed in a white Brazilian summer suit with dark Panama hat, although he secretly wished he was wearing his black SS uniform, much more impressive. Nicole was dressed in a revealing red summer evening outfit, with a large yellow flower tucked into her hair. Her makeup was impeccable, her high heels tall, and her shapely legs covered with silk stockings. Nicole was stunningly beautiful, and Axel had to keep reminding himself that she was the Scorpion and not to be flirted with.

A butler opened the front door, and the couple was shown into a parlor off the foyer. There they found Juan Perón reading a newspaper. He looked up from his armchair with an expression of surprise.

"Are we too early, Mr. Vice President?" Axel asked.

Getting to his feet, he extended his hand Axel. "I told my secretary this was to be a casual affair. Obviously she didn't listen." The two men shook hands. Then Perón gave Nicole a hug and continued, "Don't you look striking tonight, Miss López. You are a gorgeous senorita. Eva will be down in a moment. She is upstairs, freshening up."

"How many will there be?" Axel asked.

"Just the four of us," Perón answered, moving to a mahogany sidebar. "Let me mix us some drinks."

A few moments later, the parlor door opened and Eva entered wearing a white silk blouse and a yellow summer skirt. Her beauty filled the room as she greeted her guests. "Juan and I so enjoyed our lunch together that we wanted to get to know you better. I'm sorry you weren't informed it was casual. Please forgive us."

Perón handed the ladies champagne, and prepared whiskey sodas for the men. Then they walked out onto the veranda. The couples came to rest at a patio table and spent an hour, and another round of drinks, talking about the weather, world news and Argentinian politics. It was a friendly exchange, punctuated with much laughter. As the sun set, servants served a cold seafood dinner with local wines on the veranda. It was delicious and the conversation soon turned to the local theatrical scene. Eva had made a few movies and was planning on doing a play in the fall. She was a rising star, and Nicole seemed quite impressed.

After dinner, Perón invited Axel into his study for cigars and cognac, leaving the women on the patio to talk of Hollywood movies. The study was lavish, with floor-to-ceiling book shelves and a massive antique mahogany desk in front of three tall windows that reflected the rising moon. The Vice President went to a bar in one corner of the room and moved behind it.

Axel followed and took a bar stool facing him. A box of Cuban cigars appeared from behind the bar, and both men lit up. With blue smoke hanging in the air, two crystal snifters were filled with what remained of a bottle of Napoleon cognac. Perón tipped his glass to Axel. "Here's to you, Señor Garcia. Thank you for the campaign contribution. Has your ward arrived yet?"

Axel swirled his glass. "Yes, sir. On Christmas day, thanks to you." He tipped his glass to his host and took a drink. "If need arises, I would sponsor more. All I ask is no Jews, no Gypsies, and no Bolsheviks."

The Vice President chuckled. "Who the hell are you really?"

"Just a German national with a love for my people," Axel answered, puffing on his cigar.

"Why don't I believe you?" Perón asked.

"Well, sir, given the recent news from the Western Front, Germany is in a struggle for her life. Many might need my help."

That started a lengthy discussion of the war. Perón proved quite knowledgeable, and offered many opinions on the likely outcome of World War II. At one point he held up the empty cognac bottle and asked, "Would you fetch me another from the bar in the parlor?"

Axel moved across the foyer to the open door of the parlor. The room was almost dark, with only a small light burning on the bar top. He found the right bottle and turned to leave. As he did so, he glanced out to the veranda, through the open French doors. What he saw froze him in his footsteps. Nicole and Eva, standing in the moonlight, were locked in a passionate embrace. It was an unexpected scene that made his blood boil. He walked to the open door and loudly cleared his throat. Instantly, the surprised pair parted. Eva turned her frightened face to him and sobbed, "Oh God, please don't tell Juan." Then she turned and ran into the night shadows.

Nicole walked towards him, clearly angry. "What's your problem?"

"Trust your instincts, my ass," Axel blurted.

"Down here, women kiss each other," she angrily replied.

Axel approached her, tempted to slap her face. "Not the fiancée of the next president of Argentina, you arrogant bitch!"

Deception - 10 March 1945

With the muted sounds of a shower in the background, Nicole López sat on the corner of a ruffled bed, putting on her nylon stockings. When finished, she stood and straightened her blue summer skirt and buttoned her white silk blouse. With a smile like a Cheshire cat on her face she moved to the vanity, took a seat in front of a mirror, and started brushing her hair. The luxury suite of rooms, in a plush downtown hotel, was leased by the German Embassy for visiting dignitaries. She had commandeered the rooms for many weeks now. The suite made a fine love nest. Putting on her lipstick, she glared at her reflection; the hide-away was a perfect cover that no one would suspect.

From behind her, another face appeared in the reflection, wearing a white terrycloth bathrobe with a towel wrapped around her head. Eva smiled back at her in the mirror, and then placed a hand on her shoulder.

"This is a dangerous business," Eva whispered. "If Juan knew of this place, you would be dead and I would be in jail."

With a grin on her glossy red lips, the Scorpion replied, "We're safe here, sweetie. The Ambassador thinks I'm having an affair with an Argentine general. He is encouraging it, for the secrets I might learn."

"But I know no secrets," Eva replied.

Nicole stood and turned to her. "I do. Lots of secrets, enough for the both of us. I've got to go. We will leave as we always do. Same time, next week?"

Eva put one of her hands gently on the Scorpion's pretty face. "I wish I could say no, but I can't. Yes, same time, next week. But I will dream of you all weekend."

"How sweet," Nicole answered, giving her a hug. "Your scent will be with me all day."

It was just before noon when the Scorpion stepped out through the back door of the hotel and into the bright, warm sunlight. She glanced up and down the street with careful eyes, looking for any danger. The lane was parked with cars on both sides, but the sidewalks were almost empty. Satisfied, she turned to walk to the Embassy.

A burly, unshaven man in a dingy Kaiser Rambler, parked across the street, was pleased to have escaped her notice. Holding a camera with a long lens, he had taken a half dozen images of Nicole leaving, and now he waited for her to disappear before he drove to the front of the hotel, where he took another half dozen pictures of Eva departing. When he was done, he turned the Rambler for Hacienda Canario.

When the driver arrived at the villa he entered through the back door, with camera in hand, and walked to the den. Knocking on the closed door, he waited until he was instructed to enter. The room was bright, the window shutters open. Behind the desk, he found the Condor going through stacks of dispatches.

"Just like last week, Colonel. They arrived around nine thirty and left about noon. I've got them on film again. I'll develop it this afternoon," the burly driver said.

The Colonel looked up from his desk at the man. Hans Klein had been a Hamburg policeman before joining the SS in '42. He was a big fellow with broad shoulders, sandy hair and an ordinary face. Hans was the perfect detective, as he didn't stand out in a crowd. He had escaped from Italy after Mussolini was murdered, and he was a notorious SS sniper, wanted by the Allies.

"That woman is going to destroy our mission down here, damn her," the Condor answered angrily.

"If *we* know what's going on, sir, then you can bet the government knows as well," Hans answered solemnly.

"Yes, you are right. Something will have to done about the Scorpion soon. For now, however, get some lunch and then make those prints for the file," the Colonel answered.

The Condor had been busy for the past few weeks. There were now eight Canaries in country. He had purchased another safe house in the port city of Mar del Plata, and had moved U-boat Captain Wattenberg and three others into those quarters. At the Hacienda, there were now three new faces going through indoctrination. Once they were ready, he would buy another safe house, close to the waterfront in Buenos Aires, and move them there with Captain Klein in charge. The three villas would soon become the nucleus of his coming Fourth Reich.

The Colonel had not seen the Scorpion since the dinner party with Vice President Perón and his fiancée. They had had a terrible argument on their ride back to the hacienda. He had seen the two women kissing in the moonlight, and was mad as hell about it. He feared that the Vice President might find out, which could destroy his mission and be fatal to all involved. "I will go to the Ambassador and tell him of your immoral behavior," he had screamed at Nicole.

"Who the hell are you to preach morality, Colonel?" she had yelled back.

"In the camps we exterminate people like you," he had told her, and considered killing her right there in the car. But he hadn't. She still had a role to play, a purpose for her miserable life. Nevertheless, her time would soon come.

The sound of a knock at the front door roused him from his angry reverie. A few moments, later his housekeeper brought him a large manila envelope from the Embassy. He opened the manila packet and found a small wax-sealed envelope inside, dated 2.28.45. It was a fresh message from Reichsführer Hanke. Pondering whether the

Scorpion had somehow managed to read the contents before it had been delivered to him, he examined the wax seal closely. It seemed secure, but there was no way to really know.

Breaking the seal, he removed the contents of the dispatch, which included a handwritten message with two small photographs. One picture was of a futuristic-looking submarine underway; the other was the same type of boat, moored in a harbor. Both images had the words 'Type XXI U-boat' stamped on the back.

The first part of the communiqué outlined the bad news from the home front: the Soviets had liberated Warsaw, and were now knocking on the gates of Berlin. On the Western Front, the Battle of the Ardennes had failed, and Allied victory was inevitable. When the time came, the Reichsführer was preparing for his own escape. He gave no indication of how this departure would come about, but he did warn that, with the coming collapse of the Third Reich, thousands of Canaries would be heading his way. "Keep your network secured and our men standing by."

The next part of the message was a revelation. The Reichsführer told of the mission and departure of two new types of wondrous U-boats and their secret cargos. He explained that both boats carried Japanese dignitaries and German scientists, and that the Japanese government had pledged to refuel and resupply the boats after the passengers arrived safely in the Pacific. The boats would then sail east towards Ecuador. On or about May 10, the two U-boats would rendezvous at Santa Cruz Island, part of the Galapagos group of islands, some 500 miles west of Ecuador. "You will have a supply ship waiting there, with six hundred tons[5] of diesel fuel and provisions for another month of sailing for a crew of hundred twenty. One boat, U-3521, has a cargo of fifty crates of SS gold. You will upload that cargo to your supply ship and return to Argentina via the Panama Canal, while both U-boats will sail for Mar del Plata, Argentina, via Cape Horn. You are to protect your cargo at all costs. See that it is deposited into the Bank of Buenos Aires and converted to American funds. Nephew, this money is the foundation of our Fourth Reich, so be vigilant."

The last part of his orders instructed him to present the two U-boats to the Argentine government, as a gift from the German people. "Tell Vice President Perón that these new types of wonder weapons will help Argentina reclaim the Falkland Islands from the British. You will find grid coordinates and contact frequencies below. Good hunting, Hanke."

The Condor folded up the message, placed it and the photos back into the envelope, and put it on his desk. When he had done so, he stared at the dispatch a good long while. *How the hell am I going to secure a supply ship with a trustworthy crew? I'm a soldier not a damn sailor!*

Scowling, he picked up the telephone and called Captain Wattenberg in Mar del Plata. He explained his needs and asked for the Captain's advice. Wattenberg agreed to

---

[5] One Ton = 32 Gallons

do some checking on the waterfront for a merchant ship to lease, but warned that the major hurdle would be obtaining government permission to buy that much fuel and a sailing license for the ship. Due to the war, diesel fuel was being rationed all over South America. Regarding the crew, he seemed confident that he could raise enough loyal German sailors.

When the call was over, the Colonel gathered up his dispatches and moved behind his desk, where he pulled back on a hinged oil painting of the River Delta, revealing a large wall safe. Working the combination, he opened the safe and deposited the papers inside. Once he had closed the safe and repositioned the painting, he moved to the glass veranda door and looked out onto the shade-covered terrace. There, in the shadows, his three new Canaries were taking instructions from the tutor he had hired.

As he watched them, he thought about his own family. How was the Reichsführer going to escape the grasp of the Allies? And his sister in Sweden, would she be safe?

Something had to be done about the Scorpion, soon. And the government red-tape for the freighter, how would he manage that?

The sound of his phone ringing startled him back to reality. Crossing to his desk, he picked it up.

"Señor Garcia," a female voice said, "this is the Vice President's office calling. Vice President Perón would like to meet with you tomorrow at ten. Would that be a problem, sir?"

"No, not at all," he replied. "Tell the Vice President it would be my pleasure."

"Hasta mañana," the voice answered back.

Taking his seat, the Colonel opened a desk drawer, took out an American cigarette, and lit it. As blue smoke filled the little room, he wondered why Perón had summoned him. Did he know of the affair between the Scorpion and his fiancée? No, if that was the case, he would have been called upon by secret police. Maybe he had more Canaries to bargain for. In any event, he would try to enlist the Vice President's help in securing a supply ship. Should he go to the bank for more bribe money?

At ten sharp the next morning, Señor Garcia was ushered into the Vice President's massive office. He found Juan Perón seated behind his desk, in front of a large Argentina wall flag, reading from a file folder. Perón stood as he came into the room and extended his hand. "Nice to see you again, Señor," he said as the two men shook hands. The Vice President motioned to a chair in front of his ornate desk and continued, "We have not seen each other since our dinner party. I do hope that Senorita López has fully recovered by now."

Axel took his seat and replied, "Yes, sir, fully. She just had a summer cold that evening. One of those inconveniences of the season."

The Vice President took his seat. "We will have to do that again soon. Eva is smitten with your Miss López. She talks of her often. She is such a stunning butterfly, and with such an interesting personality."

"Yes, that true," Axel replied, his mind racing. "It would be our pleasure sir. Is that what you wanted to see me about?"

"No," Perón answered, his expression quickly turning serious. "I have news that might affect our German nationals. Argentina will declare war on Nazi Germany on March 25. With our upcoming elections, we feel this is the prudent policy to follow. How do you believe the German community will react to such news?"

Axel shook his head. "Sadly, it is the right thing to do sir," he finally said. "The war is lost, and now the German people must look to their future. Argentina will benefit by being allied with the Americans."

The Vice President seemed stunned by his calm acceptance of the news. The two men talked further about the news and agreed that, in the future, Argentina would have much to gain by being a member of the Allies. "The world will soon be flooded with war surplus materials that we can use in our struggle to regain the Falkland Islands," Juan Perón said proudly, his bone-white teeth flashing.

His comment opened the door to Axel's problem. "I have an uncle, on my mother's side, back in Germany," he said carefully. "He tells me that two Type XXI submarines are sailing for Argentina as we speak." Axel reached into his pocket and pulled out one of the photos. Handing the picture across the desk to the Vice President, he continued, "These boats are to be given to the Argentine people from the German people."

Perón studied the image for a moment. "Tell me about this type of boat."

Axel shook his head. "My apologies, sir, but I have little knowledge of these boats. All I know is that they are called 'wonder boats,' back in Germany."

Perón slipped the picture into his desk drawer. "I'll see what our admirals have to say about this. Now, who is this uncle of yours?"

Axel told the story he had prepared about his uncle, 'General' Hanke, and his need for a supply ship with provisions and fuel so that the submarines could complete their voyage to Argentina. He assured Perón that his South American Mining Company would pay for all costs, but admitted that he needed help securing a sailing license and permission to buy six hundred tons of diesel fuel. Throughout his explanation, he spoke in vague terms and kept many of the details to himself.

During his plea, the Vice President listened carefully, while exercising his fingers together in deep thought. After Axel finished, he nodded his head slowly and grinned. "Yes, I like it. We declare war on the Nazis and, a few weeks later, two of their submarines surrender to us! Good election headlines. Where are you to assemble with these submarines?"

"Just west of Panama, sir," he lied to the Vice President. "The freighter will return via the Canal, while the subs will arrive at Mar del Plata, via Cape Horn. But it will require a license for the ship and written permission to buy the fuel. Can you help me, sir?"

Perón tapped his fingers on his desk, his probing gaze fixed on Axel. "Yes, I will help you, Señor. This will be excellent publicity for Argentina. *But,* my involvement must remain quiet. Do you understand?

Señor Garcia got to his feet, his hand extended. "Yes, sir, I do. I will be in your debt, sir."

As the two men shook hands, Perón answered, "Yes, you will be, Señor …and someday I may ask for your help with a problem."

Axel smiled at him. "It would be my pleasure, sir."

When the Colonel returned to the hacienda, he was surprised to find the Scorpion waiting for him in his den. Wearing a conservative business outfit, she was friendly as he walked into the room. "So nice to see you again, Colonel," she said with a warm smile. "I've come to apologize for that evening at the Vice President's home. I promise it won't happen again, sir." Her demeanor seemed contrite, and Axel had to remind himself to hold back his anger.

Axel looked at her pretty face and thought, *She lies so well.* "What do you need, Nicole?" he finally asked.

"I know you received a dispatch from Germany yesterday. Was it of any importance, sir?"

The Colonel grinned at her as he took his seat behind the desk. "Yes, it was full of news and instructions, some of which are meant for you."

"What am I to do?" she asked, looking hopeful.

"You are to use your Embassy connections to buy six hundred tons of diesel fuel and thirty days of provisions for hundred twenty sailors. The Company will pay for these supplies, so the price must be rock bottom."

Nicole stood in front of his desk, looking confused. "Such purchases will require government approval, Colonel. How are the supplies to be used?"

Axel allowed himself a proud smile. "I've already secured government approval. And you will learn their use *if* and *when* you need to know. These provisions must be ready to ship out of Mar del Plata in thirty days. Do you understand?"

The Scorpion's green eyes glared back at him. "I don't like secrets, Colonel."

"Nor do I," Axel sternly replied.

Freighter Hercules - 26 April 1945

Colonel Kolb had driven to Mar del Plata Harbor early that morning with fresh dispatches, grid coordinates and radio frequencies. "Not much new information about our submarines. They are coming from Rabaul, New Guinea," he said to Captain Wattenberg on the bridge of the old freighter. "You have only a couple of weeks to reach the rendezvous point. Will you make it on time?"

"Yes, sir. We will be underway within the hour, and Captain Martin has assured me that we will be at Santa Cruz Island on the morning of the tenth of May."

"I don't like having this Captain Martin in command. You should have been allowed to be the skipper," the Colonel answered, scowling.

The *Hercules* was a six-thousand-ton freighter, owned by a Brazilian company. Senor Garcia and his South American Mining Company had leased the ship for sixty days. The terms of the lease required full payment of ten thousand dollars, a sailing license, insurance, and the services of Captain Martin and his chief engineer, as the owner's representatives. All other expenses, crew, fuel, and cargo costs were also paid by the Mining Company. The Colonel had over twenty thousand dollars invested in the resupply of the two submarines, and continually fussed over the details of the mission.

"The crew is all with us, sir," Captain Wattenberg replied. "They can be trusted to a man. We will return with your cargo safe. You can count on that."

"I trust you, Captain. It's the others who might get greedy, with tons of gold aboard. Stay alert, and monitor my radio frequency each evening. I want to follow your progress daily."

Some moments later, the departure whistle blew as the ship's motors started vibrating the decks. The two men shook hands at the rail, and the Colonel exited down the gangway. The morning dew was still on the docks as he paused by his car to watch the rusty *Hercules* lumber out into the harbor and begin its voyage north.

The old ship wasn't pretty, but she was right for the job. For over twenty years, the *Hercules* had been an inter-island, inter-country coastal freighter. The aft hull was a series of tanks which contained, that morning, six hundred tons of diesel fuel and four thousand gallons of fresh water. The forward hull was half refrigerated and half dry storage. It contained enough provisions to supply one hundred and twenty sailors for the next thirty days. The fuel alone had cost nearly three thousand dollars, and that didn't include the operating fuel for the ship. The mission was a big gamble, and the Condor was determined to protect his investment at all cost.

Opening the back door of his Mercedes, he slipped into the rear seat and ordered the driver to the Mining Office in La Plata. As the car pulled away, he removed a thermos from the seat pouch and poured himself a cup of hot coffee.

The driver, SS Corporal Kurt Hirsch, was one of half a dozen new Canaries who had arrived a few weeks before. He had worked as a clerk/bookkeeper at one of the camps in occupied Poland. After Poland fell to the Russians, Kurt had escaped through Switzerland to Lisbon. He was also a skilled typist and talented counterfeiter. The Colonel liked the kid, who spoke fairly fluent Spanish and was smart as a whip. Now the Condor had a real bookkeeper and forger in his ever-growing network, as well as six safe houses scattered around the port cities of Mar del Plata and Buenos Aires.

Much to the chagrin of the Scorpion, he had promoted U-boat Captain Jürgen Wattenberg as his second-in-command and Captain Hans Klein, the former policeman, as the enforcer of the network. The enterprise was getting so big that he had written a manifesto detailing the rules of the Argentine Odessa. Every member had signed a pledge, agreeing with the terms of the program. Behind his hacienda, he had even built a fifty-foot antenna that was connected to a ham radio setup inside his office. The Condor was ready for the flood of SS brothers who would flow into Argentina after the end of the war.

When he got to the office, his secretary gave him his messages. Nicole had called and needed to talk to him. A realtor had phoned with a new listing for a small apartment building just outside of La Plata, and Vice President Perón's office had called, inviting Senor Garcia to have lunch with the Vice President the next day.

Handing the messages back to his secretary, he said, "Call Nicole. Tell her the ship departed on time. Have the realtor send over more details on his listing, and call the Vice President's office and confirm lunch for tomorrow. Where is Vega?"

Taking back the messages, she replied with a smile, "He's in the warehouse, getting ready for another scavenger hunt."

Bruno Vega, the company's geologist, was a likable man who took long trips into the Argentine back-country in search of another great mineral discovery. Bruno knew the Condor only as Señor Axel Garcia, the owner of the South American Mining Company.

He found his geologist loading up his old Ford pickup with tools and camping equipment. "Where are you off to this time?" Senor Garcia asked.

A large smile creased Bruno's weathered face. "I'm going west. I had a revelation the other night. It was just one word – copper."

"I thought Chile had a corner on the copper market."

Vega placed an armload of tools in the back of the truck, walked to the cab, and removed a tattered map and placed it on the hood of the pickup. "Let me show you, Señor."

Axel hovered over his shoulder, watching as Vega placed a wrinkled finger on the paper. "Argentina has copper mines here, around the western town of Mendoza, but I believe that here, a few hundred miles south of the city, close to the border with Chile, there may also be rich deposits."

"Why copper?" Axel asked.

Bruno said proudly, "That was the revelation, sir. When this war is over, the world will have to be rebuilt. And what materials will be needed the most?"

"Wood and nails," Axel answered.

Vega shook his head with a smile. "No, sir. The world has lots of timber and iron. It's copper. Every one of those new buildings will require electrical wiring, wiring with copper. Copper could soon be more valuable than gold."

Axel grinned at the old man's enthusiasm. Putting a hand on Vega's shoulder, he asked, "Who owns the land out there?"

"Mostly the government, although there are some private sections around the Río Colorado area. It is a beautiful place, but out in the middle of nowhere."

"Well, Bruno, I wish you the best of digging. I will keep my fingers crossed. Maybe someday you will make us both rich men."

Axel helped the old man finish packing up his pickup, then they said goodbye and watched as the oil-burning truck rattled down the road in a cloud of white smoke. He liked the old geologist, who was the perfect front man for his company. Maybe Vega would even find something, someday.

That afternoon, when he returned to his hacienda, he found Nicole waiting for him in his study. She was in a surly mood, pacing the floor, smoking one cigarette after another.

"Colonel, I don't appreciate you not calling me back," she said as he entered the room. "Are you having me followed?"

The Condor placed his briefcase on his desk and took a seat. "No. Why would I do such a thing? I've been too busy getting the ship prepared."

"I've seen the same man, watching me from a distance, for the last few weeks now. He looks much like your Captain Klein."

"You must be seeing things, Nicole. The Captain has been working on the *Hercules* for the past few weeks. Now he's out to sea."

The Scorpion stared directly at the Colonel. "Very well. Maybe I *am* just seeing things. Do you know what happened today?"

"Yes, the German Embassy closed. Why the long face? We knew this was coming."

Nicole stopped pacing and replied sadly, "Tomorrow, all my German coworkers will board a Swiss ship and be returned to Germany. What will they find back home? Only death and destruction. You could have saved some of them for our network."

"The Odessa is only for our SS brothers. If you're sad about your Embassy friends, you should go along with them."

"You can't get rid of me that easily," she said, scowling. "With my job at the Embassy gone, I can now devote full time to our network. What will my pay be?"

"Pay? No one gets paid to be in the Odessa. You will find a job, just like everyone else."

"You pay a monthly wage to your secretary, and to that phony geologist. Why not to me? It was I who got your Odessa up and running. I know all your secrets, your safe houses, your sham businesses, and your illegal radio antenna. You need me, Colonel, more than I need you."

"A little blackmail, Nicole? I'm surprised," the Condor answered calmly, opening his brief-case. "That reminds me, the deed for our last property came in the mail today. Take a look at who owns the villa." He opened the envelope and handed the deed to her. "And you should know I have a license for the radio tower, signed by the Vice Present himself."

With a blank expression, she read the document. When she came to the last line, her mouth dropped open. It was a spot-on copy of her signature, using her German name, Nicole Lang. "How did you do this?"

With great pleasure, the Colonel said, "You might be quite surprised at the other bank records and Odessa documents that link you directly to the network. There will be no blackmail, Nicole. No threats. You are in this with us, up to your pretty neck. If the network goes down, then you go down," the Colonel concluded. Then, to drive the point home, he added, "Do you know the Grand Hotel in downtown Buenos Aires? It turns out that the German Embassy kept a suite of rooms there. With the Embassy closing, I was able to pick up the lease. It's a perfect place for our men to unwind. I'm sending three Canaries there this weekend. They will need some *Frauleins* for Saturday night." The Colonel reached back into his case and brought out another envelope and handed it to Nicole. "This should more than cover the cost. And remember, no street walkers, no Jews, no Gypsies. Use only professionals who know their trade."

Nicole was speechless, red-faced. She had lost her job, and now her love nest, and the Condor was refusing to pay her. Glaring at him, she mashed out her cigarette in his ashtray. "Shall I get you a whore, as well, or do you only prefer boys?"

With a smirk, the Colonel answered, "Not necessary. The housekeeper's daughter and I have been seeing each other for over a month now. I'm surprised you didn't know that. I thought you were the security officer."

"I will not pimp for the Odessa. That's just not right."

He smiled. "It's up to you. See to it, or board that ship tomorrow and return to Germany."

When the Scorpion departed, her mood had gone from foul to frightful. She slammed all the doors, and spun her car wheels all the way up the driveway. The Condor lit one of her cigarette butts, not sure whether she would stay or go. He hoped it would be the latter.

Later that evening, he poured himself a drink and turned on Voice of America. He could not believe the news: Adolf Hitler had killed himself by gunshot, and his girlfriend, Eva Braun, had died by taking cyanide. There was much speculation about who would replace the Führer, and what his death would mean for the outcome of the war. The

Colonel felt frozen in place. A part of him could not believe it, while another part rejoiced at this news of the Führer. The man had killed his father, and now he was dead as well. Few people in the world would mourn the passing of Adolf Hitler. Then came more bad news: German forces in Italy had surrendered, on the same day as his suicide.

He changed the station to Radio Berlin. With somber music in the background, Dr. Goebbels, the arch liar, spoke of a great man being killed with his troops while defending the Fatherland. There was no mention of the surrender in Italy. Lies, lies, and more lies. Goebbels said that Admiral Karl Doenitz would assume command of the Third Reich, but the Colonel doubted that, as well. Only an SS brother like General Hanke would be worthy of that command.

Angrily, he turned off the broadcast and turned on his ham radio set. He would need to tell Captain Wattenberg the news.

Late the next morning, Corporal Hirsch drove the Colonel to Buenos Aires and then to the address of the restaurant his secretary had written out. From the street in the theater district, the Jolie Bistro was a bizarre-looking place. The run-down, three-story brownstone had garbage cans littering the front entrance, and a black wrought-iron gate as a door. Only the faded front awning confirmed the name and address of the Bistro. The Corporal dropped the Colonel off at the curb, then parked across the street in the shade of a deserted building.

Once inside, the Colonel found a sign for the Bistro, with an arrow pointing to a dark stairwell. As he carefully moved down the narrow treads, his nostrils were struck with a strong smell of whiskey and stale tobacco. At the bottom of the stairs, he was confronted by a large, dim room with a long standup bar on its rear wall. The sides of the room were filled with red vinyl booths, with candles burning on the table tops. The center of the room offered a small dance floor, with a scattering of chairs and round tables. Only a handful of patrons occupied the tables.

The Colonel wondered whether he had come to the wrong restaurant. The last time they had met for lunch, it was at a fancy, brightly lit hotel, in a room full of admirers, not a dark and dingy bistro.

He turned back toward the stairs, then hesitated as he heard his name called out from the darkness. "Señor Garcia, over here."

Moving in the direction of the voice, he found the Vice President seated in a large booth next to the bar. He was alone, and had a drink in his hands. "Have a seat, Señor. We will get you a drink."

As Axel slid onto the bench on the other side of the booth, his eyes began to adjust. In the candle light, he could now make out Juan Perón's face. It wore a friendly expression, and the two men shook hands. "I thought I had the wrong place, Mr. Vice President. I have not heard of the Jolie Bistro before."

"It is a sentimental favorite of mine, a place full of actors, bohemians and dreamers," Juan said. "I met Eva here, a few years back. These days, we often come here after the theater."

A waiter appeared and took their drink orders. Juan requested a second whiskey sour, while Axel ordered only a beer.

"I'm surprised you're not drinking something stronger, Señor, after the recent news from Germany."

"Not many people will mourn the death of Adolf Hitler, and neither will I."

The two men talked of the war news and all of the speculation that had sprung up around it. The Vice President was pleased that German nationals had not complained loudly when Argentina declared war on Germany. "You were right when you advised me that the war was lost, and that the German people must look to their future."

The waiter brought their drinks, and the two men toasted the suicide of Hitler. It was a morbid thing to do, but the world was in a dark mood.

"So, how is your resupply mission coming? Your picture of the new submarine has my Admirals drooling."

Axel smiled proudly. "The resupply ship departed Mar del Plata yesterday morning, sir. I talked to them late last night on the radio. No problems so far."

"Good. Do you think the German crew of the submarine would help train our sailors?"

"Don't know, sir," Axel replied. "I'm sure some of the men will want to stay in Argentina. Others may want to join your navy, or find their way home. It's up to them – and, of course, up to you, sir."

The men ordered sandwiches and another round of drinks as they talked further of the future and the outcome of the war. When the food came, it was remarkably good. As it turned out, the Jolie Bistro was the best German deli in all of Argentina.

After the meal, the Vice President's mood changed. His smile became a frown, and his eyes turned to fire. "I had a more sinister reason for having lunch here today. I have a problem, Señor Garcia, and you may be able to help."

"Of course, Mr. Vice President. What is it?"

Juan slowly looked around the dark room, then reached into his suit's breast pocket and pulled out a small manila envelope. Opening it, he slid two black-and-white pictures into the candlelight.

Axel looked closely at the dim images. One was of two girls dancing together on the bistro dance floor. The other showed the same two girls kissing, under the stairwell. The girls, he saw with a sinking heart, were Nicole and Eva. His mind began to race, and his heart skipped a beat. So, the Vice President knew.

"Where did you get these pictures sir?"

"Anonymously in the mail," Juan said, quickly scooping up the pictures and placing them back in the envelope. "This is a Catholic country, Señor. Unlike Germany, it is very traditional. If these pictures got out, I would never be elected President. Your girlfriend is putting my future in jeopardy. This I cannot allow."

"She is not my girlfriend, sir," Axel pleaded. "I met her at the Embassy and had no idea of her deviant proclivities."

"For many reasons, my fingerprints cannot be on the solution to this problem. I'm taking Eva to Washington, D.C., next week, after which we will spend another week in New York City, attending the theaters. If Nicole is gone by the time we return, by whatever means, I will be in your debt. Will you help me, Señor?"

"Count on it, sir," Axel quickly replied, with the sweet taste of revenge on his lips.

Blackmail - 21 May 1945

Señor Garcia sat atop his horse, surveying the work that had been done on his property. The lower portion of land had been tilled, in preparation for the spring planting of hops, and the upper pasture was completely fenced. All he needed now were a few head of cattle and couple of additional horses to make his dream of becoming a gaucho a reality.

He spurred his mount towards the barn. The last few weeks had been miserable. First had come Hitler's suicide, then the total surrender of Germany, and last evening he had ordered Captain Wattenberg back to port. The *Hercules* had spent ten days waiting in vain. The freighter had arrived at Santa Cruz Island on time and sent out numerous radio calls for the submarines, but no response had come back. It was as if the ocean had swallowed up both boats in a single gulp. Now the Colonel had nothing: no gold for his Odessa, no U-boats to present to Vice President Perón, and he hadn't even taken care of the Scorpion as he had promised. All seemed lost.

Inside the barn, he fed his horse and brushed him down. He always thought better on top of a mount, but tonight had been different; he couldn't shake the feeling of despair. In the waning light, he walked to the hacienda and noticed a light glowing from the housekeeper's cottage. They were snug in their home, while he felt lost on his own property.

Entering the house, he fumbled for the light switch, reminding himself that all of the Canaries were gone, except for Corporal Hirsch, his driver. Still, he was confident that the villa would soon fill again with a fresh batch of SS Brothers.

As he reached his den and turned on the desk lamp, he heard the front door bell ring. It rang twice more as he hurried to the entry. "Alright, alright," he yelled, turning the porch light on.

Opening the door, he was stunned to find Bruno Vega, his geologist, standing on the stoop, carrying an armful of rocks. The man's hair was matted, his face filthy and his clothes looked like rags.

"I must speak with you, Señor," Vega said with great excitement. "This cannot wait until morning."

Axel showed him into his den, where Vega dumped the stones onto the desk. As the cloud of dust dissipated, he said, "I told you I had a vision, and here it is."

Axel stood dumbfounded, looking at the pile of rocks. Most were the size of a fist, while others were three times as big. "What the hell is this?" he demanded.

The old man picked up one of the stones and pointed to it. "See the green color of the stone? And here, the pure copper veins. These are rich beyond my wildest dreams, Señor."

Axel picked up a rock and looked at it closely under the glow from the desk lamp. It looked mostly volcanic, with a greenish coloration, and small lines that looked like pure gold in the light. It was heavy, rough and flaky. "Is it of commercial grade?" he asked, holding back his own excitement.

"I will get them assayed tomorrow," Bruno assured him, his weathered face confident. "But, from my years of experience, I say yes. I have half of a truckload outside." Reaching inside his rag of a shirt, he pulled out the tattered map and spread it on top of the pile of rocks. "Let me show you where I found these."

The two men talked for well over an hour, as Bruno explained his travels. He had searched a large area in the southern province of Neuquén, and had been lucky in stumbling across a mostly deserted valley in the volcanic foothills of the Andes. His sample rocks had come from all across that valley, and each rock had a grease pencil number that corresponded with his map, to show where the samples had been found.

On his return trip, Vega had stopped off in the capital city to look up the owners of the land in question. For the most part, it was owned by the Central Government, but three parcels were owned by private landowners. Vega thought those parcels could be purchased, for the right price.

"Have you told anyone of your discovery?" Axel asked his mind reeling.

"No, Señor. Only you."

"I'll wake my driver and we will go to the office and help you unload. Leave the map here. I wish to study it tonight."

"Sí, Señor," the old man answered, puffed up with pride.

In the warehouse, the men unloaded the samples, placing them in cardboard boxes with the correct corresponding number written on the sides. When they finished, Axel gave the old man money for gas and groceries. "Tell no one of your discovery. We will take the samples to the Assayer tomorrow morning, so be here early. And, Bruno, get a good night's sleep. You deserve it, sir."

Corporal Hirsch and Axel watched as the old man's oil-burning pickup pulled out of the warehouse. Once he was gone, the Colonel said, "We will follow him home – but at a discreet distance. He doesn't need to know."

Axel had been to Bruno Vega's home only once before. It was a rundown villa, high up in the foothills that surrounded the city of La Plata. He remembered the drive up to the hacienda as long and dangerous, with many blind curves, a good twenty-minute drive from the city.

With the pickup's red taillight some distance ahead of them, the Corporal asked from the front seat, "Why are we following the old man, Colonel?"

"I want to make sure he gets home safely – and doesn't stop along the way to blab about his discovery."

Axel's mind was still awhirl with his good fortune. Only hours before, he'd had the sinking feeling that all was lost. Now he had the copper to hang his hat on. If he could secure mineral rights on the Government land and buy up the other three parcels, his money worries would be over, and Vice President Perón would be pleased with the news of a major copper discovery. This would enrich the Government's coffers, and more than make up for his lost submarines. For all of that to work, however, the secret of the discovery had to be kept.

When the pickup turned off the paved road and headed up the gravel driveway, he had the Corporal stop his car. "Let's give the old fellow time to reach his hacienda. Then we will follow. It's a treacherous drive, so stay alert."

As they waited, the Colonel climbed out of the backseat and went to the trunk. There, he removed a small flashlight and pliers from a toolbox. On his return, he said, "All right, let's creep up the hill."

They used only the parking lights, and it was after midnight by the time they reached the hilltop. The car stopped when the hacienda was only a few hundred yards away.

There were no lights to be seen. In the starlight, they could just make out the front of the villa, where Bruno had parked his old pickup. The Colonel got out of the car and joined his driver in the front seat. All was quiet, not even a barking dog. The night was cool but clear, and stars filled the sky.

"Now what, sir?" the Corporal asked. "Should we turn around and go back down?"

"No," he answered firmly, handing the pliers and flashlight to his driver. "Go to his truck and loosen the brake lines to the rear wheels."

Even inside the dark Mercedes, the Colonel could see the surprised look on the Corporal's face. "Why, sir?" he whispered. "What has the old guy done to us?"

"Nothing at all, but he's a Jew. I won't share the riches of this copper find with non-Aryans. He has to be eliminated."

The Corporal slowly shook his head. "Sir, the old fool just made us rich. It doesn't seem right."

"This is not a request, Corporal Hirsch, this is an order," the Colonel answered angrily.

Still shaking his head, the Corporal opened his door and quickly exited.

The Colonel watched as he approached the pickup and slid under the rear of the truck. With the flashlight blinking on and off, it only took a few minutes. Then he returned to the Mercedes. "Done, sir. Should we turn and go back down the hill, now?"

The Colonel didn't like the tone of his voice. "Yes, Corporal. You have done your duty."

The next morning, Axel was at the warehouse early, looking through the rock samples and studying Bruno's old map. As he worked at writing out a packing list for the Assayer, he heard his secretary rush through the front office door for a ringing phone. She wasn't on the telephone for long before Axel heard sobbing, and then silence.

A few moments later, with an empty coffee pot in hand, she entered the warehouse for its sink. Her eyes were red, her face long. "Oh! Señor Garcia. I didn't know you were here. Did you hear the phone ring, just now? That was the police. Bruno Vega is dead!"

Axel was prepared with a look of sad surprise. "How can that be? I helped him unload these rock samples, late last night. How did he die?"

Shaking her head she replied, "Some sort of accident, coming down from his hacienda. His truck plunged over a cliff and caught fire. So sad. I liked the old gentleman very much."

"So did I," Axel answered, forcing a sober tone. "Well, we will have to find another geologist, so get some feelers out. Oh, and have my driver pull my car around. I'm going to take Bruno's samples to the Assayer. Then we'll be out of town until late Thursday night. I'll be back in the office on Friday morning."

His secretary just stood there for the longest moment, holding the empty coffee pot, as if the cold practicality of his comments had shocked her. "Yes, sir," was her only reply.

After dropping off the ten boxes of ore samples at the Assayer office, Corporal Hirsch turned the Mercedes toward the southern province of Neuquén. It would be a thirteen hour journey across the heartland of Argentina to reach the capital city. With the Colonel quiet in the back seat, studying Bruno's old map, the car sped across some of the richest land in all of South America. They passed hayfields and farms, one after another, and ranches filled with working gauchos and cattle. Colorful towns, villages, and produce stands were sprinkled here and there alongside the road. This was the underbelly of the country, the pulse of the Argentine people.

The Colonel hardly noticed the fence posts go by, consumed as he was, with plotting how best to gain control of the mineral rights for the lands of Bruno's discovery.

It was near midnight by the time they reached the capital city. It was easy to find their hotel; at five stories, it was the tallest building in town. The Colonel took a two-room suite on the top floor, while securing a sleeping room with a shared bath on the ground floor for his driver.

They spent the next morning in the Hall of Records, retrieving all of the information and necessary forms to secure the mineral rights to the lands in question. That afternoon, they drove across the province until, in the shadows of the snow-clad Andes Mountains, they found the little valley of Bruno's disclosure. They spent hours walking the property, taking pictures of the area.

With all of the proper paperwork in the Colonel's briefcase, they headed back to La Plata early the next morning. During the entire trip, the two men hardly exchanged a dozen friendly words. If Corporal Hirsch was still brooding about his role in the old man's death, the Condor couldn't be bothered to notice, intent as he was on his plotting and planning.

They arrived at the mining offices just at dusk. The Colonel had the Corporal drop him off at the front door, telling him to wait while he ran into the office to see if the Assayer's report had yet been delivered.

He found it waiting on his desk, and quickly read it in the waning light. The Assayer had written out how much copper could be produced from how many tons of ore. All ten sample areas looked promising, and he had used words like 'of commercial grade' and 'a major discovery.' At the end of the summary, the Assayer predicted that the find could be worth millions of dollars.

Delighted with the news, the Condor stuffed the report into his satchel.

It was dark by the time they drove along the hacienda driveway. The villa was as black as the sky, reminding the Colonel that it was Thursday; his household staff had the day off. He used the car headlights to illuminate the entry while he unlocked the front door and flipped the porch light on.

"Take the car around back," he snapped at his driver.

Inside, he crossed the entry and turned down the hall to his office. When he approached his den, however, he noticed a sliver of light glowing at the bottom of the closed door, and he could smell cigarette smoke.

Reaching for the latch, he pushed the door open and stepped into the room.

His desk lamp was on, and his tall leather desk chair had its back to the room. Behind the desk, he saw that the hinged painting was pulled away from the wall, and the safe open.

As he took another step, the chair swiveled around, revealing the Scorpion, dressed in her formal black and white SS uniform. She had her Captains SS hat on, with its highly polished silver Totenkopf[6] reflecting the lamplight, the desk was covered with papers and files from the safe.

In her right hand, she held a Luger pistol.

"So you are back, Condor. How nice to see you again," she said sarcastically.

---

[6] Death's head symbol

"What the hell are you doing here? And why is my wall safe open?"

A grin chased across her pretty face. "I could not resist its contents. You did have me followed, you little scoundrel."

"I never shared those pictures with Perón, but he knows. He told me so."

"Yes, I know," she said. "I sent him the pictures from the bistro."

"You what? Why? You could get us all killed."

She shook her head slowly, her green eyes glowing. "The negatives are my life insurance policy. If anything happens to me, every newspaper in the country will get prints of those pictures, along with the story of the Argentine Odessa." With her left hand, she lit another cigarette. Blue smoke hung over her hat like a cloud. "But that is your problem, Colonel. You didn't trust my instincts. When it comes to blackmail, no one plays the game better than me."

The room went quiet as the Condor glanced around, noting that the ham radio dials were lit up. "You don't have the guts to kill me," he said. "Without my bank account numbers, the Odessa is dead."

Nicole chuckled. "I knew those bank account numbers two days after our first meeting with your banker. I let him have his way with me, while I secretly took a few indiscreet pictures. The next day, when he was given the choice of me sharing the pictures with his wife or making me a full partner on the account… well, you can guess the outcome." She puffed on her cigarette. "And as to having the guts, do you recall me telling you about my good-for-nothing father who was killed by a political rival? That rival was me, at twelve years old. He had put his filthy hands on me for the last time. I shot him dead, and my mother helped me bury him before we returned to Germany. So, you see, I have no problem with killing."

"I never touched you!" the Colonel angrily replied.

"You were wise. Had you tried, I would have killed you."

Behind the Condor, the door to the study opened.

He twisted around and saw Corporal Hirsch entering the room, also dressed in his SS uniform. He was carrying a Luger pistol in his right hand. "Any problems here?" Hirsch asked.

"Yes," the Colonel answered. "Point that weapon at Nicole. She has threatened to kill me. That is an order."

The Corporal lifted his pistol towards the Scorpion, and then slowly changed its direction to aim directly at the Colonel. "All the copper information is in his briefcase. I know exactly what has to be done."

"Relieve him of it," Nicole answered.

The Corporal moved forward and took the satchel from the Condor's hand.

As he did, the Colonel glared at him. "I'm surprised at you, Hirsch. I thought you were a loyal Brother."

The Corporal grinned, moving away. "I'm done with doing your killings, sir. No more 'drive me here, drive me there.' And no more sleeping in dumpy rooms at fancy hotels. I prefer what Captain López has to offer."

"The Corporal has many hidden talents," Nicole added with a sly look, "some of which might surprise you, Condor."

The Colonel shook his head slowly and raised his hands, palms up. "Why all the uniforms? Are we going on parade?" he finally asked with withering sarcasm.

The Scorpion put her cigarette out in the ashtray. "No. I'm relieving you of the command of the Argentine Odessa." "Captain Wattenberg may well have different ideas."

"I've already talked to him. He wants no part of the FBI waiting for him on the docks. He is still a wanted felon in America, you know. He accepts my command, as does Captain Klein." Her face turned to stone, and her grip on the Luger tightened. "You are hereby relieved, Condor."

Bang.

The Colonel heard the shot, feeling his leg buckle, he started to collapse, but managed to brace himself against the back of a chair. "You arrogant bitch," he moaned.

"I will be the queen of the Fourth Reich," the Scorpion answered with a manic grin.

Bang, bang, bang. Three more hot bullets riddled the Condor's chest. He fell backwards and crashed to the floor, with a dead blank stare looking upward.

As the stench of the gunpowder cleared, the Scorpion lit another cigarette. "Strip him of his identification. Take him to the docks, weigh him down, and dump him in the bay. Then hurry back. I'll put some champagne on ice, and we will share it in the Colonel's bed.

The Corporal smiled at Captain López, "Yes, ma'am. I do love a woman in uniform." †

This excerpt was condensed from Brian's new novel *Voyage of Atonement*.

Oh, For That Right Word

After graduating from photography school, I returned to my hometown of Portland, Oregon. There I was fortunate to secure a job as a photographer for a large commercial studio. But, being the low man on the totem pole (the seventh photographer of seven) meant that all the night and weekend assignments were given to me. I did press photography at conventions, trade shows and dinner ceremonies throughout the state. I also shot department store window displays and nightclub bands. If you needed a picture in the wee hours, anytime, anyplace, I'd be there.

One of our many clients was the Oregon Ad Club. Every other Wednesday, I would photograph their luncheons in a ballroom filled with Oregon's top advertising executives. It was here that I learned of the Oregon Junior Ad Club (OJAC). This offshoot organization was for members thirty years old or younger. The club's mission was to secure worthy nonprofit clients and produce complete advertising campaigns for them at no cost. This was good for our clients and good PR for the Oregon advertising community.

CF was one of our many clients

It was the late 1960's, when the advertising industry was much like it is represented on the hit television series Mad Men, full of hard-charging, hard-working, hard-drinking creative professionals that scared the hell out of me! But, OJAC didn't have a member who was a photographer, and I was soon invited to join. After securing the blessing of my employer, I agreed.

The first meeting I attended was held in a plush conference room at one of the major ad agencies. Sitting around the large mahogany table were about twenty young fireballs, both men and women. I recognized a few of the faces but, being fresh out of school and only a few months on the job, I was intimidated by the group, so I kept reminding myself to keep my mouth shut. These folks were copywriters, artists, account executives, printers and media specialists. What the hell was I doing here?

Soon, the conversation turned to writing copy for a print ad they were doing for the client. Writing creative copy in a group is never a good idea, and this committee copywriting attempt went on and on. Before long, the group got hung up on a few words and started to argue about proper usage. Obviously, we needed a few synonyms.

Then, out of nowhere, the president of the club turned to me and asked, "What do think, Ratty?"

Floored that he had called on me, since I hadn't said a word all evening, I mustered my courage. Looking across the table I asked with confidence, "Did anyone bring a clitoris?"

Mouths dropped open and the room went silent.

The president snapped his glare back to me and asked, "What did you say, Brian?"

And, like a fool… I repeated my question, word for word.

The room roared with laughter. "I think you mean a thesaurus," the president responded, with tears running down his cheeks.

Then it dawned on me what I had said. How embarrassing! I wanted to crawl out the door and hide. But no… they were having too much fun with me.

A few years later, I became the president of OJAC, and represented the advertising community and the people of Oregon at the Paris Peace Talks during the Vietnam War. This one event would change my career forever. But that's another story for another time. During all my years with both the Junior and Senior Ad Clubs, this story of my 'wrong' word would be retold hundreds of times. *Oh, for that right word.* †

OJAC Kurt Mobley Award
1969

Charles Conkling Photographic Award
1970

American Advertising Federation
Special Project Award:
Cystic Fibrosis 1971

Chapter 13

They Shoot Horses…Don't They?

Buzzzzzz…

The loud noise from the clock radio jolted me out of a deep sleep. Reaching over to the nightstand, I turned the buzzer off and the light on. It was just 4:00 a.m., and still dark as I jumped out of bed and slid into my jeans. From the motel room next to me, I could hear my cameraman, Dick Powers, also stirring. Within the half hour, we ate a quick breakfast and picked up sack lunches from the only café in the small cowtown of Burns, Oregon. Then we loaded our film gear into a government truck and headed south, out of town. The two green BLM Suburbans that followed us down the deserted road were packed with camera crews from the three major television networks. We were all here for the same assignment: to film the first government-sponsored wild horse roundup since the Civil War.

A few weeks before, I'd received a phone call from the Bureau of Land Management (BLM) in Washington, D.C., outlining the assignment. Congress had recently passed a decree, Public Law 92-195, the Wild Free-Roaming Horses and Burro Act of 1971. Among other things, this new law prohibited the use of motorized vehicles for the hunting or relocation of wild horses or burros from public lands. Our film was to be a visual report to Congress on the practical implications of this new dictate. After resolving a few cost factors and other details for our services, I asked the BLM executive how he had chosen my company for this assignment.

In a typical bureaucratic tone, he replied, "I looked in the Portland, Oregon, Yellow Pages under 'Film Production' and saw your company's name. Media West sounded very western to me…and we're talking about wild horses…so it just seemed to fit."

Smiling, I thanked him and told him not to worry. Little did he know that my only knowledge of wild horses came from watching cowboy shows on television.

Just as the sun started peeking over the mountain tops of the eastern sky, we turned off the paved highway and bounced down a long dirt road leading to a box canyon. Here, local BLM staff had built a corral at one end of the ravine, with a high, camouflaged camera blind for the press just above it. Gathering the crews around the blind, our BLM contact explained their plans for the roundup.

It sounded simple enough. Some months before, they had found a large herd of wild mustangs in these mountainous public rangelands, some thirty miles south of Burns. For the last few weeks, the BLM staff had been driving the herd from one range to the next, always pushing them through a small canyon that was open at one end but boxed at the other. On the day of the roundup, they were moving the herd again, but this time the canyon would be fenced off so the horses would have to turn into the boxed end of the ravine with the corral.

"Will you be using real cowboys for the roundup?" one reporter asked.

"No, our staff can take care of this," was the BLM reply.

"How will we know when they're coming?" another asked.

"We'll give you walkie-talkies so you can hear the staff working the herds."

As we set up our cameras in the hot August morning of 1974, we were told that other BLM staff had arrived earlier and were already out on the high desert plains, looking for the herd. Within a few short moments, we had a line of cameras pointing in the general direction we were told that they would come from. ABC, CBS, NBC, and my two-person crew were all there, waiting to document this historic event. The corral and the hill from which they would approach were some distance from the blind, so we all used our longest telephoto lenses to fill the frame. Time seemed to drag on…until, finally, our radio came to life and we could hear that they were coming.

Moments later, on the top of a distant ridge to our left, they appeared. There looked to be forty or fifty horses, being driven by a dozen or more BLM staff. But just as the herd came into camera range, moving down the ridge towards the corral, something spooked them and they broke apart into small groups. As they scattered in different directions, the BLM 'cowboys' took out after them, galloping out of view. Soon, on the radio, we heard an update: during the chase, two of the staff had fallen off their mounts, and one needed medical attention. An hour later, when they had regrouped the herd, they tried again…but with the same results.

By the end of the day, we had only two animals in the corral—one old, gray, swaybacked mare and a lame colt! All the others had been too fast or too smart for the BLM. Using the corral as a backdrop, the network crews did the best they could at telling this nothing story. The next day, we returned to Portland and shipped off our exposed film to the BLM in Washington, D.C.

A month later, we were back in Burns to try again. This time, we came more prepared, as we had rented a 240mm telephoto lens, about the longest lens made for 16mm film cameras. The BLM was also more prepared, as they had hired real cowboys from Pendleton, Oregon. And, this time, we would be the only film crew.

Early the next morning, we were in position, waiting. With Dick checking the light, I listened to the walkie-talkie and scanned the distant ridge with my binoculars. Soon, out of a dust bowl, they came. This time, the herd looked bigger and there were only a half dozen cowboys driving them.

"Roll camera," I shouted.

In the golden morning light, we were capturing outstanding film of these real cowboys driving the wild horses. With the saddle ponies working the herd, and the cowboys yelling and snapping ropes, the wild horses moved down the ridge towards the canyon. As they went, some of the mustangs broke away, but for the most part, the cowboys were in control. With thundering hooves, in a cloud of dust, the herd soon found themselves turned up the canyon, and the corral fence was closed.

Looking down from the camera blind, I could see over forty horses now in the ravine. But the cowboys didn't stop there; riders were sent out after the few mustangs that had gotten away. A few moments later, from across the canyon and moving down a steep slope, we saw a single cowboy herding three strays.

What happened next was the unexpected and unrehearsed magic of documentary film-making. With the camera rolling, the group moved down the hill, with the cowboy's saddle pony keeping the strays together by moving quickly from one side to the other. Halfway down, the saddle pony tripped in a hole and went down, catapulting the cowboy. He turned three complete somersaults in the air and landed in a cloud of dust, on both feet, with his chaps flaring. Turning, he recovered his hat from the ground and walked back to his downed, thrashing, injured horse. Reaching to the saddle, he slid his rifle from its boot, walked to the front of his horse with a sour look on his face, and shot his mount in the head. Bang!

The sound of that single shot echoed around the canyon. Returning to his saddle, he reached down and removed it from his dead horse. Throwing it over his shoulder, he started walking towards the corral.

I looked at my cameramen. "Did you get that?"

With wide eyes, Dick replied, "Every bit."

"Grab your gear. Let's go interview this cowboy."

At the corral, we found the skinny young cowboy rolling a cigarette, standing by the fence with the wild horses in the background. Along the top rail, next to him, he had deposited his saddle. As Dick set up the camera and checked our sound gear, I asked the kid if we could interview him. He nodded yes, dusted off his chaps and put his cowboy hat on.

I started, microphone in hand. "What happen out there, this morning?"

His weather-beaten face creased as he thought for a moment. Then he replied, "Horse tripped."

After a long pause, I asked, "And then…?"

"Shot him," he answered with a deadpan face.

"What are you going to do now?"

Another pause. "Buy me another horse."

This cowboy was tall but short on words! Finally, I asked, "What do you think of the wild horses behind you?"

Without turning, he replied, "Not worth my pony."

In the end, the lanky cowboy didn't give us many words, but he did give us some great footage!

Returning to Portland, we shipped our exposed film off to Washington, D.C. Some months later, we learned that the BLM had won some type of film award for our roundup footage. We never received a copy of it for our walls but, because of our efforts, Congress amended the law. In 1976, Public Law 94-579 was passed, which allows the use of helicopters and motorized vehicles for the management of wild horses and burros on public lands. I guess it took shooting a horse to help amend the law. How sad! †

The Aloha Post Office

Soon after my wife and I were married, we moved our young family to a small suburb of Portland, Oregon, called Aloha. At that time, this area of former farmland was being developed into tracts of modest new homes. We purchased our house, three bedrooms and two bath, ranch style, for $23,000. When we moved in, we met our next door neighbors, Rick and Gayle, and their charming little daughter, Kirsten. She was about the same age of our two girls and they all soon became fast friends.

One day, while Kirsten was playing, I asked her if she had any brothers and sisters. She shook her head sadly and replied, "No, Daddy is always out of town."
I smiled at her, looking forward to getting to know Rick and Gayle better.

One Friday night, not long after our move, when I drove home from work, I found a large pile of bark dust blocking the mailbox next to Rick and Gayle's driveway. My wife Tess told me that the rural mailman had dropped off their mail with us because he couldn't get to their box.

"Why don't you call Rick and tell him we have his mail?" she suggested.

Reaching for the phone, I realized he had never heard my telephone voice before, and a prank quickly came to mind. Rick picked up the receiver on the third ring, and I heavily disguised my voice and said, "Mr. Jacobson, this is Ralph Snedley, the postmaster at the Aloha Post Office. I understand from one of my drivers that your mailbox is being blocked by a pile of bark dust. Is that true, sir?"

There was some stammering, and finally Rick answered, "Yes. I plan to move the bark dust next week."

"Well, Mr. Jacobson, that just won't do. The mail must get through," I answered, holding back a snicker. "So I've arranged for a few of our off-duty mailmen to help you move the bark dust, tomorrow morning."

There was a long pause. "Thank you, Mr. Snedley, but that's just not right. Why don't you just leave our mail with our next-door neighbors? I'm sure they wouldn't care."

Now I paused, holding back laughter. "That wouldn't be the Ratty family, would it?"

"Yes," Rick answered meekly.

I cleared my throat, trying to stay in character. "That would be impossible. Information about Mr. Ratty crossed my desk just today. He is wanted by the FBI. But you can't tell him a word of this, until we have notified the authorities. Do you understand, Mr. Jacobson?"

Without hesitation, he answered, "Yes sir, I understand. Not a word. Oh my God, you just never know."

I hung up the phone just before rolling over in laughter. Rick was at our front door within seconds, warning me that the FBI was out to get me. Soon, laughter followed and a life-long friendship blossomed, filled with love and good times. But he still hates it when I tell this story! †

Chapter 14
Savage Scavengers
Whimsical Short Story

It's a big day for Gus Savage, although, he didn't know it yet. The day had started out like any other Saturday at the Seaside Library. Most of the patrons came in early with plenty of kids in the afternoon. But now, with the warm spring weather, most readers had found their way outside. The Library closed at 6 o'clock and reopened Monday morning. This gave Gus a day and half to be with his girlfriend and hopefully muster-up the courage to ask her the 'big' question.

Gus Savage was a man of many contradictions. He looked more like a barroom bouncer, then a librarian. His stout body had muscles that oozed out of his clothes, much like Popeye from the old comic strips. His forearms were the size of most men's thighs and each had a tattoo: one was a can of spinach, the other an open book. He loved his job, especially his library kids and respected his blue-collar patrons. Yes, Gus looked more like an action figure, but deep down inside, he was gentle as a spring breeze. His only weakness was for anything in need and that even included the mangy black, one eyed, library cat.

Late in the day, in the warm and quiet library, Gus sat behind the counter, checking-in books and watching the clock. With any luck, he and Mildred would be engaged this time next week! He had bought her an engagement ring, and for umpteenth time, he looked at it again. Somehow the little diamond looked smaller and the luster of the rose setting didn't seem as bright. He fussed, is this ring good enough for my Mildred?

At the appointed time, Gus closed the library and walked outside to lock the front door. As he did, he noticed a vintage Westphalia pulling into the empty parking lot. After locking the door, he moved for the bicycle rack and saw a young lady getting out of the van and rushing towards him.

"Woo hoo, woo hoo, I have my receipt right here." she shouted.

Gus stood frozen in place with his jaw open. The approaching girl had long blue-black hair waving like a raven's wing, and looked like she just stepped out of a Barbie Book. It wasn't just her shapely figure, or her white leather boots, or even her mini skirt that caught his eye. It was her 'birds nest' hat with a stuffed roadrunner on top that made him tongue tied.

"Can I leave my VW parked here while I'm staying at the hostel?" she asked, with her green eyes flashing.

Gus shook-off his wonderment and meekly answered, "What hostel? This is public Library and we're closed."

The girl grinned with the sweetest expression, "I have rented a room here from Hostels.com, and I have my receipt. They told me you had old copies of the Seaside Signal and I need to see the April 14th 1952 edition."

Gus was enchanted, "I'm sorry missy, we don't rent rooms and we don't have old copies of the newspapers here: although, we do have back-issues on microfiche. If you come back on Monday, I'd be glad to help you."

The girl extended her tiny, white gloved hand, "I'm Lizzie Miller from Hollywood and I'll sleep in my van if I have too. But I must see your back-issues …please sir?"

Gus felt his resolve melt away like a July iceberg. He shook her soft hand and introduced himself, and then opened the library door again.

Inside, Gus showed her the microfiche reader and how to use it. She looked confused, so he sat down and searched out the right reels and loaded them into the reader.

"What's this all about?" he asked spinning through the old newspapers.

"My grandmother Jean lived in Seaside all of her life. When I was a kid, I would come here and visit her. She was a wonderful sweet lady."

"Here it is," Gus interrupted. "What now?"

"Page 4A," Liz answered, leaning over his shoulder with her jasmine perfume filling his nostrils.

Finally he found the right page. The top of the paper was sports news, while the bottom had one news story and picture.

"That's grandmother," Liz said with glee, pointing to the screen. "What's the story about?"

"A new wall safe was installed at City Hall. Jean Hastings and the Mayor are the only city employees trusted with the combination."

Lizzie stood with a big smile and showed Gus a piece of paper, "I have that combination right here. I need to see what's inside that safe. Will you help me Gus?"

Gus had been reluctant to come along, but with his basic instincts for helping and her pleading eyes, he just couldn't say no. So now he found himself riding shot-gun in her in old van and giving her directions to downtown.

"When did your Grandmother give you that combination?" he asked, watching her toothpick legs working the floorboards.

"She passed away last month," she answered with a pouty lip. "She mailed me these instructions just before she died. She said I could keep whatever I found."

"Is this some kind scavenger hunt?" Gus relied.

Lizzie sadness turned to a pleasant smile, "We won't know that, until we see the contents of the safe."

When they arrived at the old municipal building, Lizzie looked at it through the car window, "This isn't the City Hall I remember. What's happened?"

"Seaside built a new City Hall years ago. This old building is now a brew pub. When they remodeled the old building, someone might have found the wall safe and destroyed it."

"Oh no," she replied getting out of the van, "The safe has to be there!"

The safe was built into the concrete walls of the old jailhouse and no one that worked there could remember the last time it was opened. The employees guessed it was empty or that it might contain the loot from an old Piggly Wiggly robbery. In any event, the pub owner, Pete Peters, allowed Lizzie to try and open it with the combination she had. And just like magic, the safe opened on the first try. Inside she found a thick manila folder containing dozens of old photographs of Seaside and a stack of expired sewer bonds from the 1960's. The historical pictures were fascinating and the bond designs artful. The contents of the safe represented the cities bygone years.

"I'll give these old memories to the people of Seaside," Liz said, handing Gus the thick folder. "Please give her treasure to the Seaside Museum."

Gus was grateful with her generosity and asked her if she would like to stay and have a beer. She shook her pretty 'bird-nest' head and replied, "Don't drink and we don't have the time. Do you know where the Sailors Memorial is? That's where we are going next."

As they got into the van to leave the pub, Gus asked, "How did you know where to go next?"

Lizzie smiled at him, "It was written on the back of one of the photographs. I recognized grandmother's handwriting. It just read, 'Remember the Sailors Memorial and pick a black flat rock that is in the wrong place. Under it you will find the right place."

"The Memorial is at the Cove, take a left and I'll give you directions."

She started the car and they pulled out of the parking lot. "Let's go to the turn-around first."

With the radio blaring hippy songs, they drove three times around 'trails end' while Lizzie talked about the many summers she had spent in Seaside. With great fondness, she remembered the bumper-cars, the corn-dogs and the merry go round.

"From grandmothers house we could see and hear the surf. It was a wonderful home of hot clam chowder and warm love. I will miss her dearly."

"Why do you wear that 'birds nest' hat?" Gus asked out of curiosity.

"The roadrunner is the state bird of New Mexico, where grandma was born. She had them all around her house."

They finally turned for the Cove and Liz continued, "Are you married Gus?"

He blushed with the thought of his girlfriend. She wouldn't like him being here with Liz!

"No," he answered. "But tomorrow I'm going to ask my girlfriend to marry me."

"What's her name?"

"It's Mildred, she a Norwegian crab shucker."

"A what?" Liz replied.

"She picks meat from crab shells. She's the best shucker on the north coast."

"Did you buy her an engagement ring?"

"Yes," Gus answered with pride, reaching into his pocket.

He showed her the ring. She glanced at it and curled up her nose, "It's very nice... I hope she likes small things."

The well-kept roadside Memorial was just a small square pile of rocks in a sea of other shore rocks, with a flag flying above it. In front of the flagpole was a large white painted boulder with black lettering that read, 'Known only to God.' Here three sailors had died when they had come ashore in 1865. Local legend had-it that a Clatsop Indian ghost stood guard over the Memorial.

"I don't like it here," Lizzie said getting out of the van. "I came here a few times when I visited grandmother. There is something spooky about this place."

Gus joined her in front of the Memorial with a grin on his face, "Did the old Indian ghost scare you off?"

She looked up at him, with her hair dancing in the breeze, "Not all we see is reality, and not all reality is what we see. Grandma told me if I listened real closely, I could hear the Indian drums... and I did."

"Oh my God, did those drums frighten you too," Gus mocked.

Lizzie frowned, "Alright, nothing will frighten you Gus. But it did me. So let's start searching for that out- of - place black rock."

They fanned out around the Memorial, looking at a sea of rocks that all looked the same. There were big rocks and small, round rocks and flat, all in a thousand shades of different gray. It was like searching for a single dewdrop on a spring morning.

With the surf pounding and seagulls screaming, Gus was first to find it, a large black piece of obsidian surrounded by achromatic rocks.

"It's over here," he shouted clearing away the other stones.

Lizzie rushed to where he crouched with an excited face.

"Do you want me to dig it out or do you want too," he asked looking up at her.

She glanced at her gloved hands, "You better. I just had my nails done."

Gus chuckled and pulled up the flat rock. Under it he found, wrapped in a plastic sack, a tin candy box, with a color picture of an old steamship on the lid. He opened the bag and handed the tin to Lizzie. She just stood there for the longest time holding the box and caressing it with one of her hands.

"I remember this," she finally said, "Grandma always had saltwater taffy it."

Gus stood and moved closer to her, "Well open it, and see what's inside now."

The candy tin yielded the biggest treasure of them all: The front door key to her grandmother's house and a copy of her Last Will & Testament leaving everything to Lizzie. It was a teary-eyed discovery and for the longest time she just sat in her van unable to speak.

After regaining her composer, Liz insisted on taking Gus to her grandmother's house before driving him back to the library.

"I have something special to show you," she said with a twinkle in her eye.

He soon found himself waiting in the living room of a beautiful, beachfront, Cape Cod on Ocean Dr., while Lizzie searched for her special item in her Grandmothers bedroom. When she returned, she was carrying a velvet jewelry box, which she opened and showed the contents to Gus.

"Grandma had a large collection of jewelry," she said reaching for one of the many rings. "This one looks much like yours. It's a beautiful rose setting with a large diamond. I would like to give it to you for all your help." She placed the ring in his hand and squeezed his palm closed. "Mildred will like this one."

Gus was overwhelmed and moved closer to her. He mustered up his courage, and then tried to kiss her. She stopped his advance by placing a single finger on his lips and saying, "You can't do that Gus… I'm only figment of your imagination."

"Mr. Savage, I have to go."

Gus's eyes popped open and he found one of his library kids standing in front of his counter. "I'm sorry sir, I'm the last person here and I gotta get home."

With the starkness of reality, Gus nodded his approval and the young man departed. He glanced at the clock; it was just closing time. Had all this been just a dream? No, he still smelt jasmine and he noticed the ring he still held in his palm. Somehow the diamond looked bigger and the luster of the rose had returned. And on the counter, in front him, he saw the last book he had checked in, A Barbie Book!

He smiled at himself; *The library is a place where adventures come true.* †

Reunion

Class Reunion

Some time ago, my wife and I attended my twenty-fifth high school reunion at a swanky country club in Beaverton, Oregon. We hadn't graduated from the same high school and so, when we arrived at the venue, she faced a crowd full of strangers. I felt about the same, as most of the faces had been lost to the fog of time and looked very unfamiliar.

As we stood in one corner of the room, introducing ourselves to my former classmates, we were approached by a couple about our age. The lady was trim and attractive, with short, sandy blonde hair, while her husband was tall and lean. They seemed friendly enough, as we shook hands while checking out each other's the name tags.

The woman's name was Cecile, and she said to me in a nonchalant way, "I had your ring for many years, and just before the reunion I went looking for it. But I couldn't find it."

My wife glanced at me with an inquisitive expression, as long ago I had told her about my few high school romances, and Cecile's name never came up.

I looked at Cecile, bewildered, and stammered, "Ring? What ring? I just can't seem to remember."

She replied indignantly, "Our engagement ring! Can't you remember that?"

I looked at Cecile, at a loss. "Oh… our engagement ring," I answered, not knowing what the hell she was talking about.

"Well, it all turned out fine," her husband inserted. "You were going off to the Air Force, and she was just starting nursing school. So it just wasn't meant to be."

"All I wanted to do was return the ring to you, but I'm sorry, I must have lost it," Cecile added.

Smiling at the couple, I had no idea who this lady was and what she was talking about! But what could I say? Finally, I replied, "Don't worry about it, Cecile. It's a grand memory of our high school days, and I'll always remember you and what could have been."

We all laughed at the memory and the couple walked away.

This encounter did unlock a vague memory of once dating a nursing student, but wow!

How could I forget my first engagement?

Later that same evening, on the dance floor, we were approached by another couple. The woman's name was Molly, and her face did look familiar.

"Brian Ratty, do you remember me?" she asked with a friendly smile. "We dated a couple of times in our senior year."

"Yes." I smiled, proud to recall her and our few dates.

"Well, I've been mad as hell at you for years," she continued.

I stammered, again with a red face, "What did I do?"

The couple stopped dancing and so did we. "Do you remember how we drove down by Riverview Cemetery on one of our dates?" Molly asked.

"Yes," I vaguely answered.

"Out in front of the main entrance, there are hundreds of little tiny tombstones that all look alike. Do you recall?"

"Yes," I sheepishly replied.

"Well, I asked you who was buried there, and you told me it was a baby cemetery. Just the thought of all those dead babies almost made me cry! So for years, every time I drove past that cemetery, I told everyone in the car about what you told me. But my husband didn't believe you so, one time, he drove me into the grounds and proved it's a World War One cemetery. There are soldiers buried there, not babies! My friends must think me a fool!"

Another one of my tall tales has come back to haunt me, I thought grimly.

"She's always been so gullible," her husband added shyly, with a grin.

My wife glared at me with another inquisitive look, as I apologized and we danced away.

That was the last high school reunion we ever attended. There was just too damn much explaining to do! †

Chapter 15

What We Don't know!

Recently, I returned to Ketchikan, Alaska, with some pals for a salmon-fishing trip. It had been over twenty years since my last trip up, and I was curious to see how the little fishing village had changed.

On the first morning out, Skip, our charter boat guide, turned east into one of the many pristine bays of the Inland Passage. The steel-gray misty morning looked promising as our twenty-one-foot Bayliner sped past craggy shorelines and the many small islands that dot the seascape. I had been surprised to find that Skip Pattison of North-End Charters was still in business, and still using the same boat he had purchased over twenty years before. While the boat looked as fresh as the day he had bought it, what had changed was the gear that now hung on its superstructure. GPS, depth- and fish-finders, and down riggers were now part of his arsenal for catching the elusive silver salmon.

While Skip might have put on some new gear and a few pounds, his instincts for catching fish was just as I remembered. Coming to stop in a particularly beautiful cove, he soon had the lines baited and the motor trolling.

As we bobbed in the calm, deserted waters, waiting for that first fish strike, I watched the morning mist begin to roll away from the mountain tops and shorelines across the bay. Soon, out of this vale, arose two gigantic gray ghost-ships at anchor, some two or three miles across the water.

Turning to Skip, I inquired, "What are they doing out here?"

"It's a submarine base, and those are sub tenders."

He went on to explain that the Navy had built the base many years before. The government liked the location because it was so isolated and, with cloud cover 350 days a year, enemy satellites couldn't pry. Many of our nuclear submarines traveled up into these waters to have their 'acoustical footprints' tested, among other things. Fishing boats were restricted from getting too close, and the base was heavily guarded.

Gazing across the water with my mind racing, I thought, *What we don't know...*

USS Virginia (SSN-774) attack submarine

But then, what we don't know is always surprising. In 1960, when I was attached to the Air Force, learning 'Aerial Photographic Reconnaissance,' I worked on the Top Secret U2 spy plane. Before the days of satellites, this aircraft was our eye in the sky. She had a camera system that could produce razor-sharp images from a cruising altitude of over 80,000 feet. Years later, when the plane was finally announced to the general public, the government said its top cruising altitude was only 60,000 feet, and that she could only produce fuzzy images from those heights. Misinformation…What the public doesn't know can't hurt them.

Years later, on a September morning in 1981, I was driving south on Highway 95, just outside of Fallon, Nevada, heading towards Las Vegas. On one particular long, straight stretch of deserted desert roadway, my SUV became the target of two jet fighters. The planes appeared out of nowhere and dropped down to the valley floor, causing a rooster tail of dust as they came straight toward my speeding car.

With my heart in my mouth, I actually ducked behind the wheel as they swooped over my car, chasing each other. The sounds were deafening, and I could feel the heat from their engines as they roared over me. With my hands shaking, I watched them gain enough altitude to do a few barrel rolls and then disappear over a distant mountain top. Stunned, I pulled off the road and closely checked my roadmap. There it was, in bold print: Highway 95 went right through what the map called the 'Fallon Naval Range.' The Navy's TOPGUN training facility was just outside of town, and my car had just become a target of opportunity.

F-117 Nighthawk – Stealth attack aircraft

Some years after that, while driving that same highway to Las Vegas for another trade show, my wife and I stopped for lunch at the old hotel and casino in Tonopah, Nevada. The old building is a grand monument to the mining days of yesteryear. While waiting for our sandwiches in an almost deserted dining room, we overheard two guys talking at a table next to us.

One said to the other, "Did you see that sunrise over Moscow this morning? It was spectacular!"

"Yes," the other guy replied, "I was right behind you, and I couldn't believe how beautiful Moscow looked, glittering in the snow."

Finally, the first fellow sensed our meddlesome ears and lowered his tone. When my wife and I returned to our car, I asked her if she had heard the same conversation, and she confirmed it, word for word! How could two men sitting in a restaurant in Tonopah, Nevada, have seen a sunrise on that very day, on other side of the world? We found out the answer to that question a few years later when, in 1988, the Air Force introduced the general public to the F-117 Nighthawk. This Stealth attack aircraft had been manufactured by the infamous Lockheed Skunk Works, with flight crews trained at a secret air base just outside of Tonopah, Nevada. Again, *what we don't know!*

"Fish on!" Skip yelled. His shouts brought my mind back to reality, and to the pleasures at hand. Soon, with a great deal of excitement, I had my first salmon in the fish box. At the end of three days, my pals and I flew home with freezers full of fish and cameras full of memories. But I won't soon forget those two gray ghost-ships moored in that mysterious bay. How fortunate our country is to have men and women standing guard in these remote and isolated bastions of freedom. And there's one thing *I do know*…Alaska is truly a unique, beautiful and bountiful place to fish! †

Chapter 16
Tarnished Key

Mystery Short Story of Historical Fiction

Graveside: Sunday May 20, 1888

The fancy horse-drawn hearse turned off the dirt road and pranced through the open gates of the Mountain City Cemetery. Behind the carriage, a half dozen other buggies followed the somber procession into the fenced graveyard alongside the Owyhee River. The necropolis was a couple of acres of scrubland, nestled under a grove of Cottonwood trees, with numerous crude markers made of wood and stone. The Sunday morning was bright and warm, with a blue sky and puffy white clouds overhead. It was a good place and day for a funeral.

The hearse rolled up a slight rise and then stopped under the canopy of a Ponderosa tree. The tall lanky undertaker, dressed in black and with a stovepipe hat, stepped down from the carriage and dusted off his garb. Soon other guests joined the man as pallbearers and helped him remove the casket from the hearse and carried it to the plot of ground already prepared. Here they positioned the coffin on some wood beams straddling the dug grave.

Quietly and slowly, the mourners gathered around the pine box. They all looked baffled and bewildered. The Widow Reeves, with her two small children clinging to her black dress, and Doctor Meeker stood at the head of the casket looking down on it with perplexed expressions. Other grievers did the same, on both sides of the grave. Mr. Greeley, the Undertaker, stood nonchalantly at the foot of the coffin. The only sounds were the whispering of the trees in the breeze and the ripples on the river. This was a poignant moment of thought and reflection.

"Why are we here?" one of the mourners finally mumbled, breaking the silence.

Doctor Meeker raised the palm of one hand. "All in good time, Henry, I didn't really know the stranger very well. We only talked once and that was about his daughter and what happened here." The doctor was a pleasant looking, middle-aged man, with a bright mind and gentle way. His voice, after over 40 years on the frontier, still had a British accent. "Who was the first to see this bloke?"

Those in the gathering glanced at each other and then a young lad, dressed in tattered blue overalls, spoke up with a stutter, "R-r-reckon, it would be me. He and his horse rode into the s-s-stables three days ago. He s-s-said he had come from w-w-Winnemucca and was headed for w-w--Willow Springs."

"He told you his name didn't he?" The doc replied with a sharp tongue.

"Yeah," the not-so-bright stable boy answered. "He t-t-told me he was s-s-Sam, -s-Sam w-w-Woods."

On The Trail

As horse and rider came to the crest of the trail, Samuel pulled his chestnut gelding to a halt and leaned forward in the saddle to pat the mount's neck. As he did, his sharp green eyes watched three buzzards circling just off to the north. He had not seen these vultures of the sky for many years and he knew something nearby was dead or dying. Sam was dressed in fringed buckskin trousers, with a red wool tunic, a bear tooth necklace and a hand-crafted beaver hat on his head. The spring morning was cool, but clear, and the eastern trail from Winnemucca had been surprisingly good, traveling over an open prairie of sagebrush and scrub trees. He was making good time and didn't want to waste it by investigating the buzzard's prey.

"Come 'on Buck, let's move on," he said firmly to his horse, using both his voice and knees.

Like his horse, Sam was large in girth and tall in stature. At 60 years of age, he was considered an 'old man' in the company of other mountain men. His straggly brown hair and unkempt beard were peppered with gray, and his weathered face was marked with deep lines and wrinkles. But his eyes were still bright, and his body still agile after surviving the last six decades on the frontier. Samuel Woods was the best horseman, had trapped more beaver, killed more griz, and panned more gold than any other frontiersman on the Fraser River. He was a legend in his own mind and proud of it. He was the type of man that demanded respect from his friends, as well as his enemies, and had a reputation of backing up his postulates.

Sam was on the last leg of a long trip. He had received a year-old letter from his daughter Kathleen, four months before, informing him that his only son Eric had died in a mining accident. Her words were sad and short; she needed her father to come home. Kathleen was all alone on the family ranch and was reaching out to him, her last living blood relative. Her words of reunion and forgiveness had moved him, and he had finally decided to gather up his grubstake and make the long pilgrimage home.

He had walked out from Hell's Gate, on the Fraser River, to Vancouver B.C., where he boarded a steamship for San Francisco. From there he had traveled by train to Reno where he changed trains for the end of the line at Winnemucca Nevada. From there, he faced an almost 200 hundred mile ride to Willow Springs and the family homestead. It was to be an arduous trip of many months.

He had won his horse Buck, sight unseen, in stud poker game back in Winnemucca. The previous owner, a drunken pilgrim with little sense, had lost it with a full house, to Samuel's four treys. It had been a lucky draw of the cards, but then Sam had always been lucky in hunting, cards and prospecting. It was life that had always been his downfall. But now he had Buck, a beautiful ten-year-old Mustang with a blond mane, dorsal stripe and tail. This breed of horse was gentle, with great stamina and at sixteen hands tall, and a little over a thousand pounds, horse and rider were a near perfect match. Buck was, by far, the best winning hand Sam had ever drawn.

After ten hours in the saddle and with the sun shrinking, Samuel found a small grove of Cottonwoods, next to a stream, and pulled off the trail to camp. With the approaching twilight, he made a small fire and put some coffee on. As it brewed, he unloaded his bedroll and saddle bags from Buck and hobbled him in some nearby grass. As the evening chill approached, Sam squatted on his haunches by the fire and started cooking some beans. With his eyes fixed on the embers, his mind soon wandered off to thoughts of family and home. This would be a bitter-sweet reunion with his wife and son both dead and his only daughter now fully grown. He had much to atone for and feared how she might react to him.

"Hello in the camp," a deep voice from the shadows called out. "I smelt your coffee and saw your fire, can I come in?"

The voice from the dark startled Sam back to reality and he quickly stood. He glanced in the direction of the voice and found the sky filled with stars and heard the crickets and frogs singing by the stream. Slowly, he moved closer to his Winchester rifle propped against a nearby tree. "Who would you be and what brings you out here?" he answered with his right hand resting on the grip of his pistol.

"US Marshal, Red Reed of Reno, traveling from Twin Falls. Can I come in?"

"You alone?" Sam answered, with the hair on his back standing up.

"Yap, just me and my mount, who would you be, sir?"

"Samuel Woods of the Fraser River, come on in."

He heard some twigs snap and out of the shadows he watched as the marshal moved into camp leading a gray sorrel. He was covered with trail dust and had a bandana over his face. He stopped by the fire and rubbed his hands over the heat and then removed his handkerchief and brushed himself off. He wore canvas pants, a plaid shirt, and a fleeced sheepskin jacket with a shiny badge attached. As he cleaned up, Sam poured a tin cup of coffee and handed it to him.

He took a few sips. "When I saw your fire from the trail, it looked like a bear was next to it. Then I noticed that old Schofield on your hip. Not very accurate, but it has a punch."

"Killed many a griz with it," Sam said, looking the marshal over. "What brings you out here?"

"Been on the trail for almost a month... you coming from Winnemucca?"

Sam squatted, keeping a careful eye on his guest, and stirred his beans, "Yes, on my way to Willow Springs. What were you doing up in Twin Falls?"

The marshal moved his horse to nearby tree and tied him up. "Had a prisoner to deliver, never heard of Willow Springs is that up by Mountain City?"

"Don't know of any Mountain City, it was up by the Cope Ranch years ago. Would you like some beans marshal? My cookin' ain't fancy, but I got plenty."

Reed returned to the fire and took a seat on a log snag. "Sure, thanks for the consideration. I've got some bacon in my saddle bags we can add to the pot. The old Cope Ranch is now called Mountain City. Jesse Cope struck gold up there in 69." In the flickering firelight, the marshal stared at Samuel with a smirk. "Should I have papers on you sir?"

The conversation quickly turned to all business. Mr. Reed was as curious about Sam as he was about him. The marshal had long red hair, a youthful face and dark probing eyes. His lean body was muscular and his pearl handled Colt Peacemaker was strapped to his leg and hung low on his hip. Sam knew from experience that he was not a man to trifle with.

"I doubt you would. I've spent the last twenty years trapping up in BC. I'm on my way home to my family."

With his eyes still fixed on Sam, the marshal pulled out a pint bottle of whiskey and sweetened his coffee with it, "No rustlin' or killin's?"

Samuel met his glare, confident he had nothing to fear. "The only human killings I did were up in Canada. But I had good cause, and the Mounties looked the other way, because they knew the breeds I killed had it comin'. Back then my heart was filled with hate and I lived by the feud, but that was a long time ago."

The marshal's frown slowly turned to a slight grin, as he handed Sam his bottle of whiskey. "Reckon I don't have no papers on you. You can call me Red. I'll get the bacon and we can eat."

At first light the next morning, after a meal of jerky and coffee, the two men went their separate ways. The night before, with coyotes howling and the crickets chirping, they had stayed up yakking over the fire until the whiskey ran out and sleep crept in. Samuel had learned much from Marshal Reed, like why the trail was so good. A few years back oxen freight wagons had filled the way with tons of gold ore from the mines of Mountain City heading for the rails of Winnemucca.

At that time, the little city had three working mines and a population of near two thousand. Now, with just one small mine still producing, the town had busted to just a few hundred. Like so many other towns in Nevada, Mountain City had gone from boom to bust in just ten short years. It was another sad story of gold fever. But Sam also learned that ranching in the area was still good and that cattle prices remained strong. This gave him solace about his ranch and family.

Just before they rode away, they shook hands and Sam had said, "Nice meeting you Red, hope our trails never cross again…. never liked having a lawman in camp."

The marshal grinned and tipped his hat. "This country is changing, Sam. Soon all our towns will have the telegraph and then will come electrification. That will make you and I as obsolete as Daniel Boone's musket and Jim Bowie's knife. So keep your buckskins clean and your head clear. That way there won't be no papers on you."

On the slow, dusty journey east, Sam thought long and hard about what Marshal Reed had said. Deep down he knew his words were true; like the beaver, the days of the mountain man were gone. And what the hell did he have to show for his life?

Three mornings later, Sam came to the crest of the trail and found a painted sign that read: Mountain City, Pop 2050, (with handwritten numbers scrolled over it) 172. Just beyond the sign were the rooftops of a large sprawling city where the old Cope Ranch had once been. Glistening on the south side of town was the meandering Owyhee River and on the north side the foothills and crags of the Sawtooth Mountains.

From his saddle, the sea of roofs looked prosperous, but when Sam rode into town he passed building after building with blistering paint, broken windows and boarded-up doors. Where once there was commerce, now there was nothing. Mountain City was just like him - a relic from the past.

In the center of town, he found a large stable with the ringing sounds of a working blacksmith shop next to it. Here he dismounted and walked Buck towards the open barn doors.

Once inside he shouted, "Hello, anyone here?"

From the rear of the stables a tall, lanky kid appeared dressed in dirty overalls. He walked with limp and was carrying a pitchfork. As he approached he said with a stutter, "W-w-what do you need, s-s-stranger?"

"Want to board my horse overnight. What's the cost?"

The boy glanced at Buck with a scowl. "Two bits for the b-b-board, and other two bits for the f-f-feed."

Sam glared back at him, "That's twice what I paid in Winnemucca."

"That's the p-p-price mister, take it or leave it," the kid stammered.

Buck whinnied behind Sam and gave him a nudge with his nose. Sam spun around and looked at his horse with a grin. "Alright boy, you deserve it." Turning back to the stable boy, Sam flipped him a fifty-cent piece from his pocket. "Give him a good rub-down and some decent feed. He's only been eating scrub grass for the last four days."

The boy caught the coin and nodded, "You f-f-from w-w-Winnemucca?"

Sam untied his saddle bags and grabbed his rifle and bedroll. "I'm Sam Woods from way up north on the Fraser River. Would you know my daughter, Kathleen Woods? She lives up on Willow Springs?"

With a silly grin, the young man answered, "Nope, only girls I know w-w-work over at the Ponderosa and n-n-none of them are named Kath-l-leen."

Sam shook his head. The kid wasn't very bright, and had nothing to offer. "Is there a post office in this town?"

"Yep, across the s-s-street at the m-m-Mercantile; Mr. m-m-Mitchell is the owner, the postmaster and the m-m-Mayor. Hell, he e-e-even owns the Pon-der-osa."

Graveside

A bullfrog, down among the river reeds, croaked out his haunting call, while a red-tailed hawk added its high-pitched call from high above the Ponderosa tree.

"Who saw him next?" Doc Meeker asked his neighbors.

The invited mourners glanced again at each other, not sure who should answer. "Reckon, that was me and my missus," Mr. Mitchell said. "He walked into our store looking and smelling like a bear. I hadn't seen a mountain man in years, so he caught me off guard."

"I was stocking shelves when he came in," Jean Mitchell added, "about fell off my ladder when I saw him. At first I thought he was some Indian looking for trouble."

"There are lots of ruffians out here, what made him so different?" Doc Meeker asked.

The Letter

With saddle bags and bedroll on his shoulder and rifle in hand, Sam walked into the general store across the street. It looked and smelled just like most stores on the frontier. It was a large room with a potbelly stove in the center, surrounded by tables filled with merchandise. On one side of the room were shelves of dry goods and clothes. On the other side, was food and sundries. The back wall had bins of hardware and a long wooden counter with an ornate cash register and gold scale.

Sam found the proprietor behind a table, sorting fabric bolts. Being the only customer in the store, he walked over to him and introduced himself. "I'm Samuel Woods from up on the Fraser River, would you be the mayor and postmaster?"

"Reckon so, and part-time constable," the man answered with some hesitation. He was small, with a slender face, and rimless spectacles resting on a large, bony nose. With his gray eyes, he gave Sam a nervous look. "What can I do for you?" he finally asked.

Sam dropped his traps to the floor, rested his rifle on the counter, then reached into his pocket, and brought out the folded letter he had received from his daughter. Opening it, he handed the letter to the proprietor. "Was this sent from here?"

The postmaster gazed at the envelope, which had six five cent black stamps attached and examined it up close to his glasses. "Yes, this was mailed from here. It has the city mark. Is there a problem?"

He handed the envelope back and Sam pointed to the return address. "It's from my daughter, Kathleen Woods. Do you know her? Is she still living up at Willow Springs?"

The postmaster shook his head. "Don't recall her. But then I don't much look at people mailing letters. All I care about is if the postage is correct."

"She'd be 29 now," Sam added. "A pretty girl, with blond hair and deep green eyes. Sure you don't recall her?"

"No," the man answered shaking his head again.

From across the room a middle aged lady stocking shelves called out, "I think I remember her." She stepped down from her ladder and walked towards the men. "I'm the Postmistress, Jean Mitchell. She came into the store one stormy night, well over a year ago, and asked how much it would cost to send a general delivery letter to Prince George, Canada."

"What did she look like?" Sam asked.

The lady smiled warmly, "Just like you said, blond, pretty with deep green eyes. But I don't recall her name as Kathleen Woods. She told me her name was Kathy McKee. I remember it because she was short three cents for the postage and started to cry. So I took what money she had and mailed her letter. Only talked to her that one night."

Samuel reached into his pocket and took out his coin purse and placed three pennies on the counter. "Thanks for your kindness ma'am. She must have gotten married while I've been gone. Do you know if she talked to anyone else in town?"

She nodded yes, "Saw her the next morning talking to Doc Meeker on the street. When I looked up again, she was gone."

"Where could I find him?"

"He came in for coffee this morning," she answered. "He told me he was going out to the Jenkins Ranch to help deliver a colt. The doc is a creature of habit, so you might find him at the Ponderosa this evening."

Sam nodded, "Thank you ma'am. Is there a hotel in this town?"

"Yes," the postmaster answered. "On the main trail, just east of town you'll find the Ore Hotel. It takes in miners, cowboys and roughnecks. Not the best place to stay, but better than campin'."

"That's a horrible place," Mrs. Mitchell said with frown. "He should try at the Cope Boarding House; it's just down the street."

Mr. Mitchell shook his head, "The Widow Reeves won't rent to miners, cowboys, or Indians. A mountain man like him would scare the hell out of her two children."

Sam felt his anger boil up; how dare he say anything about the way he looked! But then he noticed the lady nodding in agreement. "My husband's right, Sam," she said with that same friendly smile. "You'd need to clean up and get some new clothes. We're not in the wilderness anymore."

Sam glared at the two shopkeepers with anger in his green eyes. No one up on the Fraser River would ever talk to him like that. But then, he wasn't on the river anymore, he was back in polite society again. So he relented. "I'll put myself in your hands ma'am. Dress me up the best you can."

That's how Sam's revival started. Jean Mitchell took him over to the dry goods and started picking out clothes for him. With her nose twitching, she did all the selecting and sizing. But, because of his ripeness she wouldn't let him put any of them on until he had bathed. Sam hadn't been around a white woman for a long time, so it was a joy to watch her work. The only other woman to ever fuss over what he wore had been his wife Sarah, many years before.

When they were done, Sam paid her $5.45, the most he had ever spent for store-bought clothes, and then she directed him to the local barbershop and baths a few doors down from their store.

Graveside

"That's when I first saw him," a tall, well-dressed man with a waxed handlebar mustache said standing near the grave. "When he came into my shop, he looked and smelt like a pigsty. It took two tubs of soapy hot water before I'd touched him with my scissors. But when I was finished, it was the best transformation I had ever done. He went from a moth to butterfly in less than a half day."

"Wish I could have seen him," Jean Mitchell added. "I liked him, mountain man or not."

The barber chuckled, "When I was done with him, I asked if I could look at his teeth. He bolted out of my chair like a bullet, yelling, "Why? My teeth ain't got no hair.""

The assembled mourners snickered, after which the stable boy asked, "Did he leave you a t-t-tip?"

"Yap, a silver dollar," the barber answered proudly. "And he bought one of my bottles of hair tonic. I told him it was good for his scalp. Guess he doesn't need it now."

Doc Meeker cleared his throat and raised an eyebrow. "I wouldn't be telling folks that story. Maybe it was your tonic that killed him. Who saw the stranger next, after he was all cleaned up?"

With a sad face, and in a near whisper, the Widow Reeves said, "He showed up at my front door that afternoon. When I first saw him, he looked like a rancher."

"Louder... we can't hear you," one of the gathered shouted.

Mrs. Reeves, with her hair dancing in the breeze, pulled her two children closer to her. "We talked awhile on the front porch," she said with more authority. "He told me, he was searching for his daughter and needed to talk to Doc Meeker later in the evening. So I rented him a room. I liked the man."

The View

When Sam was done at the barber shop, he departed with his head chilly, his body cleansed and feeling a little naked without his beard. The barber had given him directions to Reeves Boarding House and had told him that the widow, for a fee, would wash and clean his old clothes. "She takes in boarders and laundry. It's the only way she can feed her two children," he had said casually while cutting Sam's hair.

As Sam walked toward the boarding house, in his new store-bought clothes, he kept glancing at his reflection in the few shop windows that weren't boarded up. Jean Mitchell had done a fine job in selecting a denim outfit with a dark blue cotton shirt. But it was the black felt Stetson on his head that he enjoyed the most. If only his old mates on the Fraser River could see him now!

Just across the street from the Ponderosa, and next to a boarded-up church with a tall steeple, Sam found the home of Mrs. Reeves. The two-story Victorian had a white washed picket fence in front and a large, welcoming front porch. The house seemed out of place, surrounded by other buildings and shops that were all closed up.

Once on the porch, Sam saw a small sign, in a front window, that read: Room to let. He straightened his hat, and knocked on the front door. After a second knock, the door opened and a handsome middle-aged woman, dressed in a flowered frock and white apron asked, "Can I help you, sir?"

She had long auburn hair, pulled back in a bun, with hazel eyes and a creamy complexion. Samuel introduced himself and asked if he could rent a room. Mrs. Reeves seemed friendly enough. She asked a few questions about why he was in town. He answered all her queries and told her about his search for his daughter.

"Jean Mitchell, at the mercantile, told me Doctor Meeker was the last to see her. I hope to meet him tonight at the Ponderosa and find out more."

The widow frowned, "The Ponderosa is the devil's den," she said. "But Doc Meeker is a good man." With that said she invited him into her house and agreed to rent him a room. In the kitchen Sam met her two children; Nancy was six years old and standing on an apple box rolling out dough, while Matthew was eight and also standing on a box, picking at a chicken carcass. They seemed like nice kids and very polite.

"Is there a school house in town?" Sam asked Mrs. Reeves.

She frowned, "Not anymore. The town couldn't afford it"

Then they went upstairs and she showed him his room at the back of the house. The chamber was bright and tidy with a large brass bed and a big window that overlooked the river. And just down the hall there was an indoor bathroom, a new invention he had not seen before.

"I'm afraid I've never used such a place," Sam said shyly.

"I'll send Matthew up. He'll show how it all works," the widow answered with a grin.

The cost for all this luxury: a dollar a night, plus four-bits for two meals and extra two-bits for his laundry.

That evening he went down for dinner before going to the Ponderosa. At the table, he met the other three boarders living in the house. Two older sisters that talked like magpies, and an old gentlemen with white hair, sad eyes, and an ear trumpet. No one seemed curious about Sam so he sat back and enjoyed Mrs. Reeves chicken and dumplings - the best he had ever tasted.

It was dark by the time he left the boarding house. As he crossed the street, he noticed how dark the town was. Other than the lights from the saloon, only a few other buildings and homes had lamps that could be seen. Even the cities gaslights no longer worked. The town was as dark as a coal mine and as quiet as a tomb.

When he walked into the Ponderosa he found a large barroom, filled with round tables and wooden chairs resting on a sawdust floor. The room smelled of sweat and spit and on the back wall was a long mahogany standup bar with brass spittoons and a footrest. Behind the counter was a long mirror with rows of bottles and on the walls, paintings of nude women. At one end of the room was a piano, at the other end a staircase leading up to the girls cribs. It was a typical saloon with only a few drinkers and two bar girls huddled around tables.

Sam approached the bar and ordered a whiskey. "What's with the boarded up church across the street?" he asked.

A burly bartender, with garters on his sleeves, poured his drink and replied, "We used to have three churches, now we don't have none. The miners ran the last preacher out of town and the city boarded up his church. Guess it's the sign of our times."

Graveside

"That's when I first saw him," Ralph Brooks, the Bartender from the Ponderosa, said. "He told me he was looking for the doc, but he hadn't been in yet."

"I'd been out at the Jenkins ranch all day helping with some livestock," Doc Meeker inserted. "I didn't know the bloke was looking for me. What else did he say to you Ralph?"

"He was curious about Mountain City and what is was like back in the boom days. He bought me a drink and we talked awhile about the town and his ranch up on Willow Creek. He told me he was looking for his daughter, and that the doc had talked to her last, and he wanted to learn more. That's about when you came in doc."

Doc Meeker nodded sadly, his eyes fixed on the coffin before him. "Yep, he was filled with questions about his daughter. She was a tragic patient I remembered only too well. In my heart, I didn't want to tell him, but I had to. But I didn't want to talk about her in front of you Ralph. News like this should come only face-to-face and man-to-man.

So I asked him to join me, at a table, in the darkest corner of the bar. Here I told him what no father ever wants to hear..."

Crossroads

Later that night, when Sam walked back across the street to the boarding house, his mind was a sea of sad memories. He hadn't cried, he hadn't gotten drunk nor had he blamed any one for anything. He was just numb and lost in a world of long ago.

As he climbed the front steps to the porch, he found Mrs. Reeves reading a book in the lamplight. He nodded at her, without a word, and moved towards the front door.

"Did you see Doc Meeker?" she asked in a whisper.

He stopped and turned back to her. She was seated in a wicker chair alongside a wicker table. Even in the dim lamplight Sam could see her inquisitive face. "Yes," he answered with one hand on the door latch.

"What did he tell you?"

Sam wasn't sure he could tell her. "What are you reading?"

She smiled at him and placed her book on the table. "It's our family Bible. I try to read it each night, when the house is quiet, and kids are down. What did the doc have to say?"

Sam turned back to the door in near tears. "Not much."

"It's better to talk about it, Mr. Woods, I've learned that from experience."

Sam turned and took a step towards her. "He told me my daughter was dead," he answered with choked-up voice. "She died while giving birth to her stillborn baby about a year ago. There was nothing the doctor could do for her or her baby. She just g-damned died!"

With his profanity, the chill of death swept over the porch and Sam stood frozen in place with an angry face. Mrs. Reeves glared back at him with pity.

"Come sit next to me," she finally asked gesturing to the empty chair next to her. "I lost my first child when we moved out here. She would have been ten by now. Then three years ago, my husband Harry died of pneumonia. This is a hard country, Mr. Woods. Tell me about your daughter."

There was something special about Mrs. Reeves. The way she looked at you, the way she talked. She made Sam feel safe. So, with his head still spinning, he took a few steps and sat down. "My wife Sarah and I lost our first child at birth as well. I know only too well how hard it can be out here. But my daughter's death is all my fault."

"How could that be?" the widow asked.

Sam hung his head and started talking like he was in a daze. "Were do I start? A long time ago, my son Eric and I were returning to our ranch after a day of hunting. When we approached the house we could see two men ransacking it. Once they saw us coming, they lit-out on horseback. Inside the house, I found my daughter Kathleen hiding in the root cellar under the kitchen. Her mother, my wife Sarah, had told her to hide there when two Indians had come knocking on the door looking for food. She offered them what little bit we had, but they wanted more and started beating the door down. That's when she hid my daughter in the cellar." Sam stopped, with his hands trembling. He remembered that dark day like yesterday.

"How old was Kathleen?" Mrs. Reeves asked in a whisper.

Sam shook his head, not wanting to revisit the truth. "She was nine, and Eric fifteen. After removing her from the cellar, I started searching and calling for my wife. But there was no answer. That's when I sent the kids outside. Moments later, I found Sarah upstairs, naked and dead. She had done her best to fight them off, but in the end, the breeds had raped her and slit her throat... and just for spite, they cut-up her chest."

Mrs. Reeves reached for her tattered Bible and placed it back in her lap. Then he heard her horrified question. "Why would they do that?"

Sam lifted his head and stared right at her with his green eyes glowing with fury. "They made tobacco pouches out of her breasts."

"Oh, my God," the widow mumbled.

He looked away again, "For the longest time, I just stood there in our bedroom, looking down on my wife's mangled body. That's when I realized that I wasn't feeling grief, only hate. Her death was my death, her killers were mine and I would never rest until I had my revenge.

The next day, we carried Sarah's body to the Cope Ranch in our buckboard. They were our closest neighbors and dearest friends. We buried her in their family plot, down by the river. After the funeral, I took my children aside and told them that I was going after the Indians that had killed their mother."

"Weren't they a little young Mr. Woods?" the widow interrupted.

"Yes," Sam answered shaking his head. "But I was only fifteen when my father died and I became the man of the house. Still, my children were confused; they didn't understand my anger or my need for revenge. So I gave them what money I had, and told them to go home and take care of the ranch, then I lit-out to find the breeds. That was twenty long years ago."

"Did you ever find them?"

"Yes. It took me a year, but I tracked them to Canada. They turned out to be brothers, and I slit both of their throats. God forgive me, I enjoyed it."

Mrs. Reeves shook her head and said softly, "Vengeance is mine sayeth the Lord."

"By then I was just a hollowed-out shell of a man, and only wanted the solitude of the wilderness. So I fell in with some mountain men who taught me how trap and prospect. That's where I stayed for all these years."

The porch went quiet, with only the sounds of the crickets down by the river. Sam was still lost in his thoughts, carrying the grief for his daughter. "Kathleen sent me a letter, when I was still up on the Fraser River. It was a year old by the time I read it. She told me my son Eric had died in a mining accident and asked me to come home. I agreed, but I took my own sweet time getting here. Just this morning I learned Kathleen had married when I was gone and was now called Kathy McKee. Then tonight the doc told me her husband had died in the same cave-in that had killed my son. She had lost her brother and her husband in that same filthy gold mine up in Oregon." Tears finally stung his cheeks and he sobbed, "She didn't even know she was pregnant when they died."

The widow glared upon him with sad eyes, "You're a big man with a good soul Mr. Woods and the Lord loves good giants. Maybe this will help," she whispered, handing him her Bible. "It did for me, when I lost my Harry. Take it with you to your room, and put yourself in God's hands."

Sam looked up at her with a tear stained face and slowly nodded. She seemed like an angel of reason.

Graveside

"I saw him early the next morning saddling up his horse at the stables," the Blacksmith Tom Taylor said. "He looked like a sad man with a blank stare. We didn't talk; he just saddled up and rode away."

"Does anyone know where he went?" Doc Meeker asked.

"I do," The Widow Reeves answered. "He told me he was going out to the cemetery to see where his daughter was buried. I offered to go with him, but he wanted to be alone."

Yesterday and Today

In his mind, Sam remembered exactly where his wife had been buried twenty years before. But when he came to the old family cemetery everything looked different. The sign out front called it The Mountain City Cemetery and the plots were spread out on a couple acres of land. The trees were taller and fuller, and the only landmark that seemed the same was the Owyhee River. He searched down by the river and close to a tall Ponderosa tree before he finally found his wife's grave. Her weathered wooden marker was faded with her name almost unreadable and weeds had taken over all around her grave.

At first he just stood there, looking down at her plot, remembering the love they had shared, the strength of their union, and the dreams they had dreamt together. It was a flash of memories of when the family was strong and their future bright.

Then he collapsed to the ground on both knees and started to sob. "I have been adrift without you…you were always my rudder, you were always the voice in my head and my guiding light. I have nothing without you."

Samuel Woods remained on his knees, talking to his wife until he could sob no more. Then he walked the grounds looking for the fresh marker of his daughter. He found it in a sparsely used area with a good river view. But the marker said, Kathy McKee. Sam frowned on that idea; she had come into the world as Kathleen Woods, and would go out the same way.

He knelt next to her marker and asked her for her forgiveness. "I should have come home long ago. I'm sorry about your baby, your husband and brother. I pray for your forgiveness. We will all meet again in the in the sweet by-and-by."

Sam stood, and in that fleeting moment, he knew exactly what had to be done.

Graveside

"He came into our store early that afternoon," Jean Mitchell said. "He bought a bolo tie with a sliver clasp of a buffalo and some writing materials. He seemed friendly enough, but a little distant. When I complimented him on his new clothes, he smiled and called me ma'am again."

"Who saw him next with his new tie?" the doc asked.

"He came back into my shop," the barber said. "He was wearing his new tie and wanting another shave. But this time, when I finished, he wanted the lilac water."

"Did he say anything about where he had been or what he had done?" the doc asked.

"No," the barber answered. "He only wanted to know where he could buy a good beef steak dinner. I told him the Ponderosa."

For a moment the grievers didn't say anything and then the tall lean Undertaker, Gill Greeley said. "I must have seen him next; he smelt like lilac water and had that tie on when he came into my parlor. He was the most bizarre client I've ever had."

Farewell

Sam found the undertaker's parlor just off the main street and next to a small barn. The storefront had two windows with closed coffins standing upright on the inside. One was draped in black and had a sign: 'Blaster Jeb Johnson, viewing 10 cents.' Sam bristled as he walked through the door.

In the rear of the shop, he found Mr. Greeley, with hammer and gouge in hand, working on a wooden marker. Sam approached him and said, "Why do undertakers like you prop up the dead in their windows for money?"

The lanky mortician brushed off the wood chips from his apron. "He was a pauper and it's the only way I get paid for my services. Why would you care?"

Sam shook his head sadly, "It's just not right." Then he introduced himself. "I've got some good business for you," he said. "But we have to come to an understanding first."

"What kind of understanding?" the undertaker asked.

Sam glared at the man, "There will be no viewing of my body, no mention that I was a mountain man, none of your embalming fluids in my veins or that I was the giver."

"The giver of what?" Mr. Greeley asked with a curious face.

"Never you mind," Sam answered, handing him a written list of things that had to done. "If you prop me up in your window, or change these instructions in anyway, I'll come back and cut off your nuts and use your sack as a tobacco pouch! Do we have an understanding?"

The undertaker felt a chill race through his body. He had never been confronted by such a big man, with green eyes, that glowed with anger before. "Yes, we have an understanding," he finally relied.

"Good," Sam said. "Now what will be the cost?"

Mr. Greeley read the list twice, his hands quivering. "A funeral, four grave plots side-by-side, the moving of two graves, two new pine coffins: one for you, and one empty, in the memory of your son, and a large stone marker with the names and dates of your family… hum, forty five dollars should cover it."

"Good," Sam answered reaching into his pocket.

With the undertaker's eyes still fixed on the list, he said with excitement, "Mr. Woods, you have your name listed here with your date of death as tomorrow. We should just leave that blank."

Sam glared back at him again and handed him the money, "Don't change a thing. Your work must be completed by Sunday morning. Now show me your stones and I'll pick out the marker."

Mr. Greeley's jaw dropped. "For ten dollars more I can provide you with a linen lined mahogany coffin…"

Graveside

"It was late in the afternoon when he arrived back at my boarding house," the Widow Reeves said. "I was in the kitchen cooking when he came in. He told me he was going out for dinner and would be late. Then he talked with my children about their old school house and what they liked about it. He seemed very interested in what they had been learning. Then he told me he was going upstairs to take a bath. As he turned to leave, he said, "The future is with our children. I wish I would have realized that many years ago. Thank you for the loan of your family Bible, it is like you, full of wisdom and strength." Mrs. Reeves lowered her head, "Those were the last words we had together."

"Are w-w-we about done?" The stable boy Jerry stuttered. "I've got s-s-stock to f-f-f-feed."

"Yes," Doc Meeker answered holding up the palm of one hand again. "There's only one more bit to this tragic riddle. Did he come into the Ponderosa that night?"

"Yep," Ralph Brooks the Bartender said, "walked in about eight o'clock. He ordered a bottle of whiskey and a steak dinner. He was all dressed up and looked as healthy as horse. He sat all alone in the same corner as you did with him doc. There was nothing unusual about it."

"Anyone else talk to him that night?" the doc asked looking around at the mourners.

One of the girls from the Ponderosa, Laura Hope, cleared her throat, "I did," she said meekly. He bought me a drink and I watched him devour his dinner. He didn't say much, but I had the feeling he liked having me around."

Final Farewell

That night, Sam walked into the Ponderosa without his pistol. He had reminded himself he wasn't looking for any trouble, only a good time and good eats. When he came through the saloon doors he found the bar crowded with miners and cowboys. It was a payday Friday for most of the men still working in the dying town.

Pushing his way to the bar, he ordered a bottle of whiskey and asked the burly bartender, "How long ago was the preacher run out of town?"

The barkeep shrugged his shoulders, "Two or three months ago. Why?"

"Just curious," Sam answered over the noise of crowd. "I want the steak dinner with all the trimmings."

The bartender nodded and brought out his bottle of whiskey and placed it on the bar. "Find yourself a table and I'll send someone over to get you set up. It will take some time for the dinner."

Sam nodded and pushed his way back through the crowd. With the bottle and a glass in hand, he searched the room for an empty table and soon found the same dark corner he had shared with Doc Meeker the night before. Here he sat down and poured himself a drink. With the piano player banging out barroom tunes, Sam relaxed and watched the coming and goings of the boozers and losers. It was a fascinating study of the human condition for a group of total strangers he would never see again.

An hour later, when he was just finishing up his meal, one of the bar girls approached his table. "Hey mister, will you buy me a drink?"

For the longest moment, she just stood there in her green velvet, ruffled dress, with black stockings, looking down on Sam. He enjoyed the view with a wide smile and finally gestured to an empty chair. "Sure, why not."

From the moment her ass hit the seat, she started talking about herself, the other men in the bar and her dreams of being a show girl in San Francisco. Sam didn't say a word; he just listened and poured the drinks. It had been a long time since he had been with a white woman, so he just let her ramble on.

After she finished her second drink, she gazed at him in the candlelight and finally asked, "Do you want a poke, cowboy?"

Sam smiled at her. She was a tiny woman with a busty figure and a pretty painted face. But he had known all along, that sooner or later, the proposition would be asked. "Sure. What would be the cost?"

"You're a big man mister and I don't want you on top of me. Let me do the work."

Sam nodded, "And the cost?"

"Two dollars' worth of enjoyment you won't soon forget."

Sam grinned; he knew full well that she had inflated her price because he was a stranger and so big. "Sure. Why not."

With the bottle half gone, Sam and the lady went upstairs. Once inside her crib, she wanted to take care of business first. So Sam reached into his pocket and handed her a Ten Dollar Gold Eagle. The amount of the coin gave her pause, "I don't have any change for this. We don't see many gold eagles here."

"It's all yours," Sam answered. "All I want is conversation. I want to watch you brush your hair, smell your perfume bottles and have you tell me about your family. That's all."

With an inquisitive face, the bar girl sat down on the foot of the bed. She seemed a little frightened with his proposition, could she trust this big stranger? But slowly her fear turned to comfort and they spent the next few hours just talking together. When Sam left her room, he thanked her, and told her it had been an enjoyment he won't soon forget. She blushed and gave him a hug.

Graveside

"He wasn't my ordinary gent," Laura added with a smirk. "But he was a true gentleman."

"I remember now," the bartender added. "He came downstairs just after midnight and bought a pint of brandy from me. Then he paid his tab, and walked out the door."

The doc used a handkerchief to wipe sweat from his forehead. "Did anyone else see him after midnight?"

Everyone looked at each other with blank stares. "Margaret, why don't you tell them what happened next." The doc said.

Mrs. Reeves had stood with a sour face, with all the talk about the Ponderosa. She hadn't liked it. Now her eyes came alive and she spoke with authority. "I didn't hear Mr. Woods come home that night. And Saturday morning he didn't come down for breakfast. So I told my son Matthew here," she said, putting her hand on his head. "To go up and see if he was alright. Moments later, he yelled for me and I rushed upstairs. Inside his room, I found Samuel slumped in a chair, in front of an open window. His eyes were closed and he looked like he was in a peaceful sleep. I shook him, but he didn't wake up. He was dead. Then I sent Matthew out to fetch Doc Meeker and Mr. Greeley.

While I waited, I just stood there looking down on poor Mr. Woods. That's when I noticed a few things. On the table, next to his chair, was his pistol and next to it was my family Bible. On the top of it was an envelope with my name on it. It wasn't sealed, so I opened it and found a note inside with these." The widow reached into a dress pocket and brought out two paper bills. She held them up so the people could see them. "Two five-hundred dollar gold certificates," she said with humility.

The mourners let a gasp; no one had ever seen paper gold certificates before.

"Here's what Mr. Woods wrote in his note:

I leave to Mrs. Reeves, and her two children, this money and the deed to my ranch up on Willow Springs. May she and her children take root up there… it's good bottom land and a great place to grow a family.

I give her this property, and money, as payment for her hospitality and spiritual advice that helped me find my way. God bless her and her family

Samuel Wood's
May 19, 1888"

The gathered were stunned by Sam's words and money. Some looked down on his coffin, while others just stood there shaking their heads.

"Margaret showed us the money and the note, when Mr. Greeley and I we got there," Doc Meeker added. "I examined Mr. Woods; there was no blood, no bruising, no cuts. No signs of foul play. On the table next to him was his old Schofield pistol, halfcocked, but not used. And an empty bottle of brandy, but with no signs of poisoning. It looked as if Mr. Woods had just up and died! I told Mr. Greeley we would take him back to his parlor where I could do an autopsy. But we didn't find anything."

"Tell them about the key doc," Mrs. Reeves said.

Doc Meeker nodded, wiping his forehead again. "As we waited for help to move Samuel, Margaret picked up her family Bible and this key dropped out." He reached into his vest pocket and showed everyone a brass key about three inches long. "And, when she opened her Bible, she found another envelope inside."

"It was right there in Romans 12:19," Margaret said with pride.

"Anyhow," the doc continued. "It's addressed to the people of Mountain City, and Samuel asked its contents be read at his funeral."

Doc reached in to his coat pocket and showed everyone the sealed envelope. He opened it and read it aloud:

"I appoint Doctor Meeker and Mayor Mitchell as the trustees of this, my last will and testament. The key is for lockbox #314, which you will find at the Wells Fargo office in Winnemucca. The box contains what remains of my grubstake from the gold fields up on the Fraser River. This tarnished key and the iron box represents the worst of me and my wasted life. But in the memory of my daughter, and with the spirit of

this frontier town, I have restored my faith in God and pray for a brighter future for all. Therefore, I hereby bequeath the contents of the box to the people of Mountain City. May they find success and happiness where I have found none. The city needs a church, a schoolhouse and street lights that work. Without God, books and light, Mountain City is just another town of failed dreams.

Samuel Woods
May 19, 1888

PS: Give my horse and traps to the stable boy Jerry; he has a good way with Buck. And don't forget the city cemetery... it needs maintenance."

The mourners around the open grave just stood in quiet reflection for a moment. Then the blacksmith blurted, "Sounds like a lot of money, but how did he die doc?"

The doctor looked bewildered. "I wrote on his death certificate natural causes. And nothing I've heard here this morning is going to change that. I think he just willed himself to die. The cocked pistol was just there in case he needed it."

"He died of a broken heart," the Widow Reeves said.

"He was a strange man," the bar girl replied.

The widow answered her with a sharp tongue, "He was a good Christian man with a big heart! That's how we will remember Samuel Woods." †

Ten days later, Doc Meeker and Mayor Mitchell, returned from Winnemucca with the contents of the lockbox: $55,547.00 in gold and silver certificates, two rawhide pouches of gold dust and nuggets, the deed to half ownership of a producing gold mine on the Fraser River and a Daguerreotype of Sam and Sarah's wedding. The original iron lockbox, the picture and the tarnished key can still be viewed today at the Pioneer Museum in Mountain City Nevada.

**Wilderness
Trail
Trivia**

Those that drink whiskey with the owls at night cannot soar with the eagles the next day.

Horse Trivia
A horse's brain is only the size of a man's fist, but its heart is the size of melon and can weigh more than nine pounds. - A horse's ear is always pointing to where they were looking. - In a single day, a horse could drink up to ten gallons of water and defecate up to fourteen times. - A horse only needs two hours of sleep a day, and most of the time they sleep standing up.

Trail Recipes
Frontier grub includes such foods as sourdough biscuits, buffalo jerky, spruce beer, pig knuckle stew, beaver/squirrel meat and pickled salmon.

Frontier Homilies
By 1860 most of the coastal Indians were gone. They had either died from European diseases or been forced to move to reservations. The Columbia River, without Indians, was like the night sky without stars. †

Acknowledgments

Special thanks to my editor's Judy Meyers, Katie Miller and Jan Bono. My long-time story editor Judy helped me with many of the stories contained within. Katie edited and proofed many of my new short stories as well as the galley for this manuscript. These professional editors make me look good with their special talents for the English language. And to my favorite editor Tess, she has read, corrected and made invaluable suggestions for all my books. Hat's off to all!

My Bride

I met my wife Tess, while working as a commercial photographer in Portland Oregon. She worked in the advertising department for a major department store. Her job was to give me merchandise that needed photography for newspaper ads. Not so exciting items, such as tableware, pots, pans and silverware. At the time, little did we know how our friendship would grow.

In many ways we are as different as fire and ice. She is quiet and unassuming, I am not. She is generous, I am stingy. She sees good, where I see trouble. But when it comes to our core values; faith, country, family, friends and dreams, we are rock solid. And that's the blessing of our near fifty years of marriage. Our love is a language only spoken by our hearts. She makes me be a better man! God bless my bride.

Why Historical Faction

Good historical faction enlightens and entertains. The characters within the story, real or imagined, are the glue that holds the storyline together and moves the plot forward. While the events (who, what, where, when and why) tie the story together and then hopefully provide an exciting and memorable read of history.

This method of writing is not a genre, but a technique of storytelling that dates back to earliest forms of verbal and written communications.

My Books

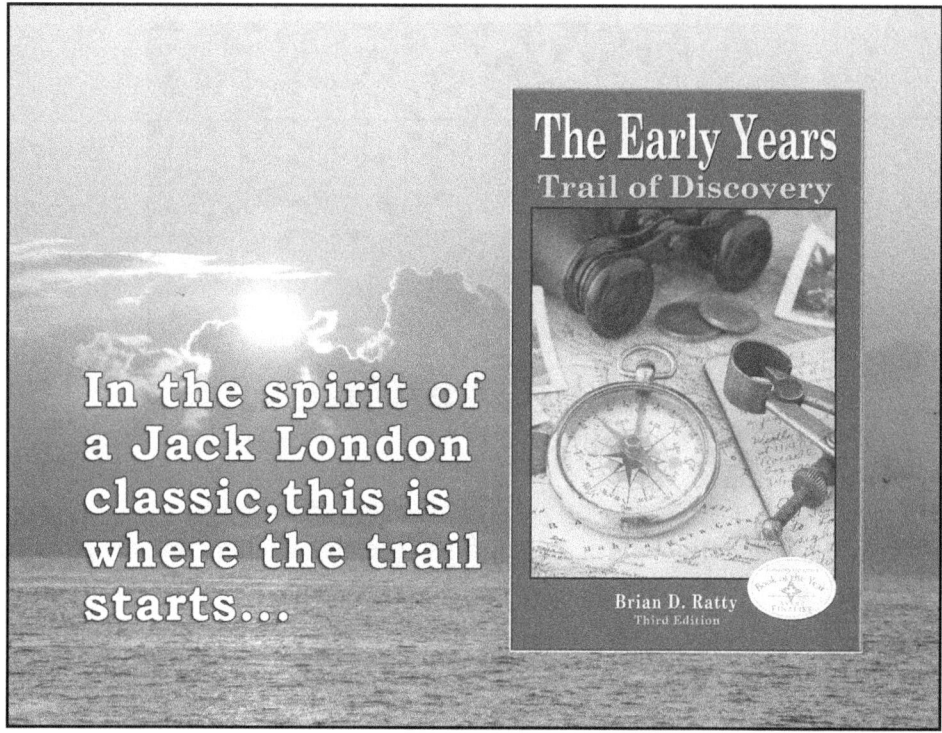

The Early Years: Trail of Discovery (Third Edition)
ISBN: 978-0692254721

We all come into this world alone, and go out the same. Between coming and going, is life. **The Early Years** is a story about life and how a yearlong adventure defines the future for a young man named Dutch Clarke.

Manipulated by the terms of his dead Grandfather's will, Dutch undertakes a one-year ordeal in the rugged wilderness of British Columbia in 1941. This is a classic story of one man's personal struggle to come of age against all odds.

Dutch begins his trek accompanied by his horse Blaze, two mules and a half wild dog, Gus. As they pack into the remote Nascall Valley, he digs deep, learning courage, self-reliance and how to survive. On this unforgiving trail, Dutch faces many obstacles, some life threatening, some inspiring and all a challenge to his character and spirit.

Froward Magazine Book of the Year Finalist

My Books

The War Years: Through A Bloody Lens (Second Edition)
ISBN: 978-0615987286

In 1942, as American blood is about to be spilled in far off Guadalcanal, a young man boards a train and blindly heads towards his destiny: boot camp with the United States Marine Corp. These tragic times were the defining years for millions of American plowboys and cowboys. **'The War Years'** is a compelling chronicle about these years and one not so ordinary young man.

Dutch Clarke, over the objections of his prominent family, answers his country's call. Just as he is about to complete boot camp, family influence steps in and propels him through the ranks and into the Office of War Information. Here he puts down his rifle and takes up photography.

Working with a former TIME Photographer and a Nikkei Cameraman Dutch learns the power of the lens and the courage to use it. The **'The War Years'** is a uniquely different war story about men who fought their way across the Pacific, not with guns but with cameras. This tapestry covers more than just guns and bullets: it also about prejudice, friendship and the ultimate sacrifice.

Froward Magazine Book of the Year Winner

My Books

Tillamook Passage: Two worlds - one destiny (Second Edition)
ISBN: 978-0692259351

Joseph Blackwell, a lad without prospects, befriends a mysterious sea captain and secures a berth on his ship. The year is 1787, and two American ships laden with supplies set sail from Boston Harbor. Their venture: to round Cape Horn and sail to the Northwest coast of America, to trade with the Indians for sea otter pelts.

During their stormy passage, the two ships lose contact with each other. As a result, Captain Robert Gray, must proceed on his own. Reaching the Northwest coast, they discover native villages on a large, pristine bay which Gray names after the Indians: Tillamook.

Tillamook Passage a rare view into early years of the Oregon Coast. Native Americans rarely take center stage in historical fiction with strong maritime themes, but Tillamook Passage is an exception. And the author, Brian Ratty, adds an even rarer element, the unique native cultures of the Pacific Northwest coast, which have deep sea traditions and technology that still amaze modern mariners. Tillamook Passage explores this history more deeply than almost any other historical novel.

Eric Hoffer Literary Award Winner

My Books

Destination Astoria (First Edition)
ISBN: 978-0615940779

In 1809, ruthless businessman John Jacob Astor schemes to send an overland expedition to the mouth of the Columbia River. **Destination Astoria** reveals the remarkable odyssey of one young fur trapper, Dutch Blackwell, who joins that enterprise.

From Boston, Dutch travels cross-country with his dog and his horses to meet up with Astor's brigade in St. Louis. Along the trail, he encounters Mountain Jack, a seasoned frontiersman. The two men form an alliance, forsaking the Astorians, and cross the continent together.

During their tormented passage, the men face death from starvation, dehydration, searing heat and Indians both hateful and helpful. Crossing the uncharted wilderness becomes the ultimate test of their tenacity.

Destination Astoria, an enthralling story steeped in history, moves across the unforgiving heartland with the force of a prairie storm. With vivid descriptions, thoughtful characters and brutal twists, the story portrays a lost breed of adventurous frontiersman who helped blaze the Oregon Trail.

Readers Favorite Five Star Winner

My Books

Voyage of Atonement (First Edition)
ISBN: 978-0692454282

In turbulent 1963, a grieving Dutch Clarke turns his sailboat sextant towards the Pacific and starts a quest for life's age old question: *why*. Along the way, he is joined by three other crewmembers that are as quirky as the times. These adventurous souls will face the perils the Pacific and chase their unforeseen future over the next dark horizon.

Voyage of Atonement is a thrilling novel about sea scavengers who stumble across a mysterious entombed U-boat with a cargo of Nazi gold. This revelation sparks the vicious reaction from a secret group of former Nazi SS members (ODESSA) and the newly formed country of Israel. These conflicting interests soon turn their discovery into an international spy thriller with deadly consequences.

Will these four scavengers do the right thing? Will they face the future with clear minds or suffer Years of Atonement for the sins of their decisions?

Readers Favorite Five Star Winner

Brian D. Ratty is a retired media executive, publisher and graduate of Brooks Institute of Photography. He and his wife, Tess, live on the north Oregon Coast, where he writes and photographs that rugged and majestic region. Over the past thirty five years, he has traveled the vast wilderness of the Pacific Coast in search of images and stories that reflect the spirit and splendor of those spectacular lands. Brian is an award-winning historical fiction author of six novels and the owner of Sunset Lake Publishing.
For more information: **www.DutchClarke.com** and **www.facebook.com/Dutch1942**

www.ingramcontent.com/pod-product-compliance
Lightning Source LLC
Chambersburg PA
CBHW080832250626
47160CB00008B/2911